DISCUSSIONS OF LITERATURE

Discussions of
SHAKESPEARE'S

HISTORIES:

Richard II to Henry V

Edited with an Introduction by

R. J. DORIUS, *University of Hamburg*

D. C. HEATH AND COMPANY
BOSTON

PRINTED JULY 1968

CONTENTS

INTRODUCTION

Shakespeare's English history plays reflect complicated elements in his background and his art: considerable reading in Sixteenth Century chronicles and other sources; inherited attitudes toward the English kings and their reigns, which helped to determine the limits and richness of Shakespeare's approach to his materials and his audience's response to them; an Elizabethan world-picture or climate of related ideas and opinions—political, religious, and philosophical, learned and popular—which Shakespeare draws upon and in turn develops; contemporary dramatic and literary conventions, at once a discipline and a resource; and Shakespeare's own restless artistic and moral energies, perpetually seeking new forms for new meanings. From the earliest of these histories (parts of *Henry VI* are at least as early as 1591) to the last (*Henry V*, 1599, if we exclude *Henry VIII*), these nine plays form the most sustained and penetrating study of the uses and abuses of power in dramatic literature, and a remarkable preparation for Shakespeare's treatment of the relationships between private man and public figure in the heroes of the tragedies.

Readers of the last four of the histories—*Richard II* through *Henry V* —concern themselves sooner or later with a number of related questions: To what degree do these plays, or two or three of them, form a "unity," in over-all conception, in design, in effect, or thematically, in the recurrence of images, characters, or related scenes? To what degree do Shakespeare's histories form a separate genre, containing elements of both tragedy and comedy and possibly of epic, differing in proportion with each play? How can we know the basic assumptions of such a genre, as mixed as that of the problem comedies, so that we can respond to it on its own terms? Is *Richard II*, for instance, with its variety of tones and styles, rendered more or less unified by such a generic hypothesis? Is Henry V seen more appropriately as the ruthless man of power or as the "mirror of all Christian kings"? And are we to respond to Falstaff grimly or merrily? Is he a devil of the moralities or a contagiously persuasive figure of "festive" comedy? Of course the complexity of Falstaff and of most of the problems discussed in this anthology renders it difficult, if not absurd, for us to be content with simple answers, or even to pose our questions in terms of simple antitheses or polarities. A familiarity with attitudes current in Shakespeare's age, and particularly with those revealed in his other plays, is essential in helping us to cope with such questions. But as in all of Shakespeare, each of the histories establishes a language and an organizing center of its own. A close reading and rereading of these plays, therefore, before and after a sampling of criticism, can help us best in our attempts to determine basic assumptions as they emerge in plot, interaction of characters, and texture of language.

The essays collected here suggest various, often contradictory, ways of thinking about these plays. The primary emphasis is upon critical writing of the last twenty-five or thirty years, during which the histories have greatly benefited, as has the rest of Shakespeare, from recent bibliographical, historical, and "new critical" studies. This little anthology begins and ends with essays which suggest helpful over-all approaches to the plays. Rossiter's lecture points out the doubleness and complexity of all characters and events in the histories. Sewell is concerned with limits and controls in the interpretation of character. Developing a similar position historically, Langbaum rounds off the essays on *Henry IV* by pointing out the problems we face, as inheritors of romanticism and of a literature and criticism which emphasize point of view, relativism, and psychological interpretations, in understanding Shakespearean character primarily in terms of plot and action and the governing direction of a play. And Stoll, writing somewhat earlier, underlines the role of dramatic convention and of the expectations of audiences in Shakespeare's day.

The writers who are concerned here with Falstaff represent, with Coleridge, a main line in the interpretation of character in Shakespeare, from Johnson and Morgann in the Eighteenth Century, through Bradley in the early Twentieth, to Stewart, whose essay provides a helpful summary of attitudes toward the rejection of Falstaff. From the beginning, commentators on the histories have been aroused to passionate gestures of defense, dismay, and rage by this rejection and all that it implies for the interpretation of these plays and Shakespeare's dominant ideas or attitudes. Much of the controversy has revolved around Morgann and later Bradley, with their emphasis upon character and "real life." Against these writers, Stoll and others, emphasizing dramatic convention, have long waged total war. To see the play of critical methods in the writing on the histories at its fire-cracking best, one should follow up the writers (whether here or elsewhere) whom many of the critics here employ as foils for their thinking, as Langbaum and Sewell, for instance, employ Morgann.

Other critical approaches are also represented in this volume. Jenkins and Leech are concerned with structure; Rossiter, Leech, Williams, and Sewell with tone or atmosphere; the present editor with image and theme; Stewart with myth and symbol; Langbaum and Stewart with changing attitudes toward Shakespeare; Rossiter, Langbaum and Sewell with theoretical positions and problems. The best Shakespearean criticism, as is evident here, employs several methods and cannot easily be categorized. No net catches more than a few fish, and thus many kinds of nets are necessary. With a few notable exceptions, criticism of the histories still awaits the kind of synoptic view exemplified by the Rossiter lecture which opens this volume. A lively response to essays on these plays, therefore, will question them constantly, employing them not as final judgments but as possible ways of seeing and understanding. The more suggestive the essay, the more insistently important questions should arise. Of Langbaum one might ask, for instance, whether Shakespeare's world is in all ways "absolutist," whether at least it is in this respect substantially the same as Dante's, and whether the tragedies do not in fact question the governing values they seem to assume.

To supplement these essays, the student will wish to consult the book-length studies of the English histories that have appeared in the last two decades or so by Tillyard, L. B. Campbell, Traversi, Ribner, and Reese, some of the writing referred to in the survey of work on the histories in *Shakespeare Survey 6* (1953), essays on these plays in the J. Q. Adams Memorial Volume (1948), and also more recent criticism, some of which, like C. L. Barber's excellent essay on the Saturnalian element in *Henry IV*, has been reproduced too frequently to be included in this collection. Further reading in historical criticism, as in the introductions to these plays available in the *New Cambridge* and *New Arden Shakespeares,* will help to deepen the readings assembled here.

A brief list of suggestive titles follows:

Barber, C. L., *Shakespeare's Festive Comedy,* Princeton, 1959.

Campbell, L. B., *Shakespeare's Histories,* San Marino, 1947.

Cunliffe, J. W., "The Character of Henry V as Prince and King," *Shakesperian Studies,* ed. Brander Matthews, New York, 1916.

Empson, William, "Falstaff and Mr. Dover Wilson," *The Kenyon Review,* vol. XV, no. 2, Spring 1953, pp. 213–266.

Granville-Barker, H., *From Henry V to Hamlet,* Oxford, 1925.

Mahood, M. M., *Shakespeare's Word Play,* London, 1957.

Reese, M. M., *The Cease of Majesty,* London, 1961.

Palmer, John, *Political Characters of Shakespeare,* London, 1945.

Ribner, Irving, *The English History Play in the Age of Shakespeare,* Princeton, 1957.

Stoll, E. E., *From Shakespeare to Joyce*, New York, 1944. *Shakespeare Studies*, New York, 1927.

Tillyard, E. M. W., *Shakespeare's History Plays*, New York, 1946.

Traversi, Derek, *Shakespeare, From Richard II to Henry V*, Stanford, 1957.

Wilson, J. Dover, *The Fortunes of Falstaff*, London, 1944.

R. J. Dorius

notes on the
CONTRIBUTORS

Andrew Cecil Bradley (1851–1935), English teacher and Shakespearean critic, is remembered chiefly for his *Oxford Lectures on Poetry* (1909) and for *Shakespearean Tragedy* (1904).

Samuel Taylor Coleridge (1772–1834) developed his ideas on Shakespeare chiefly through lecturing. The passages included in this volume are from the notebooks of about 1810, the lecture notes of 1811–1812, and the *Literary Remains* of 1836.

R. J. Dorius, currently guest Professor of English at the University of Hamburg, edited the Yale edition of Shakespeare's *The Life of King Henry the Fifth* (1955).

Harold Jenkins is Professor of English at the University of London. In addition to *The Structural Problem in Shakespeare's Henry the Fourth* (1956), he has also published *The Life and Work of Henry Chette* (1934) and *Edward Benlowes* (1952).

Samuel Johnson (1709–1784) published his influential *Preface to Shakespeare* in his edition of the plays in 1765. The passage included in this volume is from the fourth volume of this edition.

Robert Langbaum is Professor of English at the University of Virginia. He is author of *The Poetry of Experience: The Dramatic Monologue in Modern Literary Tradition* (1957).

Clifford Leech is Professor of English at the University of Toronto. Among his most recent books are *John Ford and the Drama of His Time* (1957) and *Shakespeare: The Chronicles* (1962).

Maurice Morgann (1726–1802), an eighteenth century lawyer, is remembered for *An Essay on the Dramatic Character of Sir John Falstaff* (1777).

A. P. Rossiter (d. 1957) has written *Angels with Horns and Other Shakespeare Lectures* (1961) and *English Drama from Early Times to the Elizabethans: its background, origins, and developments* (1950).

Arthur Sewell has written *Katherine Mansfield; A Critical Essay* (1936), *A Study in Milton's Christian Doctrine* (1939), and *Character and Society in Shakespeare* (1951).

J. I. M. Stewart is currently at Christ Church, Oxford. In addition to *Character and Motive in Shakespeare* (1949), he has written *Montaigne's Essays: John Florio's Translation* (1931), *Eight Modern Writers* (1963) and many detective novels under the pseudonym Michael Innes.

Elmer Edgar Stoll (1874–1959) was Professor of English at the University of Minnesota. Among his most influential studies are *Shakespeare Studies* (1927) and *Art and Artifice in Shakespeare* (1933).

Charles Williams (1886–1945) was a novelist, critic, and playwright. The critical study *Reason and Beauty in the Poetic Mind* was published in 1933, and a collection of his *Selected Writings* appeared in 1961.

William Butler Yeats (1865–1939), the Irish poet, playwright, critic, and essayist, wrote of Richard and Henry in "At Stratford on Avon," which appeared in *Ideas of Good and Evil* (1903).

A. P. ROSSITER

AMBIVALENCE
The Dialectic of the Histories

First, my Feare: then, my Curtsie: last, my Speech. My
Feare, is your Displeasure: My Curtsie, my Dutie: And
my Speech, to Begge your Pardons.

If you looke for a good speech now, you vndoe me: For
what I have to say, is of mine owne making: and what
(indeed) I do say, will (I doubt) prooue mine owne
marring.

But to the Purpose, and so to the Venture.

STRATFORD 1951, a Shakespeare Memorial Theatre playing a sequence
of History-plays in a fixed unchanging Elizabethan-house-front stage-set.
Stratford 1612, a man writing his last History: *Henry VIII*, first performed 29 June 1613, when in a sense it "brought the house down,"
for The Globe was set on fire. . . . And as far as I know, no Shakespeare
History-play was staged with Elizabethan décor—or non-décor, if that
suits you better—till this year, 1951. We should hope to find *some* cur-
tains taken away (from the mind, I mean), *some* unanticipated continui-
ties revealed, *some* unexpected groupings, interconnections, echoes. . . .

The Man was 48; had begun writing Histories some twenty years
back, perhaps as early as 1586, when he left home and twins, and was
perhaps "a Schoolmaster in the Country" (as Beeston jun. told Aubrey).
How did he *end* by thinking of History? Had he any coherent "view"
of the Historic Process: from John—with a jump to Richard II (1398)
and thence more or less consecutively to Bosworth and 1485, the Tudor
dawn . . . ?

His last play—or his and Fletcher's—ends with the dazzle of the Elizabethan sunrise: with the christening of the baby Elizabeth, and Cran-
mer in the role of "prophet new inspired." Yes; but in 1612 the Queen
was nine years dead; the great age was dying before her; and this Man,

From *Angel with Horns* (1951), pp. 40–64. Copyright Longmans, Green & Co., Ltd. 1961.
Reprinted by permission of Theatre Arts Books, New York, N. Y. The version reprinted here
has been somewhat abridged.

who had seen so deeply, so terrifyingly, into human experience could not be blind and deaf to the *ironies* of his last stage-situation. To say no more: Could he, who had staged so many "poor painted Queens," be nescient of the irony of Anne Bullen's triumph—he knowing all that followed . . . ? And with the noble, pathetic, fallen Katherine in the self-same play?

Looked at *one* way, the Histories present a triumphal march of the destinies of England. But look at them another way—at the individual lives of men and women—and your conclusion will be nearer to what Yeats wrote (also *At Stratford on Avon*):

> He meditated as Solomon, not as Bentham meditated, upon blind ambitions, untoward accidents, and capricious passions; and the world was almost as empty in his eyes as it must be in the eyes of God.

I find that apposite to the Histories; for though Shakespeare gives but few generalizations applicable to "the Historic Process" (as we grandly call it . . .) yet Yeats catches the note that rings beyond the melancholy brooding of Richard II on the fates of Kings: the note of the helpless Henry VI at Towton (Pt. 3, II. v); it is near to the feeling of Henry V's "idol Ceremony" speech; it generalizes for Margaret of Lancaster, for Isabella of France, for Katherine of Aragon . . . (Proud Names!) . . . for all the long line of women broken in the course of great events. And it most precisely fits that generalizing moment when the weary sleepless Henry IV is turning over in his midnight mind the history of his own times:

> O God! that one might read the book of fate,
> And see the revolution of the times
> Make mountains level, and the continent,
> Weary of solid firmness, melt itself
> Into the sea . . . how chances mock,
> And changes fill the cup of alteration
> With divers liquors! O, if this were seen,
> The happiest youth, viewing his progress through,
> What perils past, what crosses to ensue,
> Would shut the book and sit him down and die.
>
> (Pt. 2. III. i. 45.)

Those melancholy tones are familiar enough: they are what makes the burdened man-beneath-the-Crown a major symbol in the Histories. The voices murmur on behind the tapestries: "sad stories of the deaths . . ." "all murdered . . ." "Upon the King . . ." "Uneasy lies the head . . ." They mind me of Chaucer's lines (on quite another theme):

> What? Is this al the Ioye and al the feste?
> . . . Is al this peynted proces seyd, alas,
> Right for this fyn?
>
> (*Troylus and Crysede* ii. 421 f.)

But though there is a "Doubleness" here: in the conflicting values set by the Greatness (the Triumph) of the National Destiny, and the Frustration, the inadequacy, of the Individual (the frail Man within the robe)—there is nothing complex in that "Doubleness." It falls just short of the tragic; where Man's greatness is asserted in his destruction. That falling-short is characteristic of the Histories.

These kings and great persons are all sub-tragic. They lack a degree (or some degrees) of freedom; are caught in nets of events by which they are frustrate and less than their potential selves. In Rilke's phrase, they are *Verwirrt mit Wirklichkeit:* bondsmen to a "reality" which is that of the world of action, therefore temporary, pragmatic, unreal. And they (to quote Yeats again):

> Constrained, arraigned, baffled, bent and unbent
> By those wire-jointed jaws and limbs of wood,
> Themselves obedient,
> Knowing not evil and good;
> Obedient to some hidden magical breath.
> (*The Double Vision of Michael Robartes*)

The mechanism to which they are subjected is that process of "retributive reaction" which is the only *tragic* component of the Histories.

Retributive Reaction is my name for the principle of the simplest of the patterns in these plays; of which pattern we see only a short and misleading section in the Richard-to-Henry V tetralogy. *There,* the usurpation of Bolingbroke (exactly described in terms of consequences by Carlisle), with Richard's death by murder, leads on to the Unquiet Time of Henry IV—to the Percies' Rebellion, and the father's fears that Prince Hal is just another Richard; and so up to the death-scene in "Jerusalem" and "God knows, my son . . ." followed by the advice to "busy giddy minds/With foreign quarrels": which is—despite all that Archbishops may say—the political reason for Henry V's French campaign. That is victorious, and the curse of usurpation seems to sleep. Yes, to *sleep;* it is not dead.

The closing chorus of Henry V refers back to the Henry VI series, the loss of France—"which oft our stage hath shown." Thus the sequel to *Henry V,* in the complete pattern, is "Hung be the Heavens with black" and the Roses series, where "civil dissension" carries forward the curse of royal murder, uncertain or divided right, brother against brother, for the sixty years to Bosworth Field.

The pattern can be extended the other way, to *Henry VIII* (I mean in Wolsey as antagonist to Katherine, and what we know of Anne Bullen, the usurperess). It is one of Shakespeare's constants. But when I say "retributive reaction" I mean just that; for whether it is "justice" or not, God knows . . . (Professor Butterfield would have it that *he* knows too, and that it *is* all the Will of God. To me, it is obscure, ironic, *and*—as far as Shakespeare shows me the scheme of things—seemingly end-less.) Taken all together, the Histories are a dark glass, where we gaze *per speculum in enigmate.* The mystery beneath the surface of the magic mirror with its shows of kings is chill and deeply saddening.

> Action is transitory; a step, a blow,
> The motion of a muscle, this way or that,
> 'Tis done, and in the after-vacancy
> We wonder at ourselves like men betrayed;
> Suffering is permanent, obscure and dark,
> And shares the nature of Infinity.
> (Wordsworth: *The Borderers*)

This pattern of "obscure tragedy" runs, for me, far deeper than any feelings *I* can derive from knowing the "philosophic" system which modern scholarship has extracted from the plays (and other Elizabethan sources *undique coemptis*). I must briefly outline it, (*a*) because it is indubitably "there" as a pattern of thought, and (*b*) because it offers simplifications which are in danger of diminishing the true complexity of Shakespearian History—and in the best plays. Remember, then, that I am *not* arguing anything *away:* a pattern is *there,* and it is like Ed-ward Halle's. But Halle's theory of history is naïve, and though the Elizabethan reader found it as satisfying as the Chronicles of Israel and Judah (with similar formulae on how King So-and-so did that which was evil in the sight of the Lord and followed after the ways of Jeroboam the son of Nebat who made Israel to sin), yet I cannot find it in my reading of Shakespeare to suppose that his mind was quite as naïve as all that. There is more in the dark glass than the moral history of the Lancastrian House of Jeroboam and the happy ending in the dawn of Tudarchy.

On Order, Degree, and so on, let me be brief: the essentials only need recall; let me remind you:

The State, as monarchy, is ordained by God; its structure is hierarchi-cal, and in health all its orders or degrees are "congreeing in a full and natural close/ Like music" (as Exeter says in *Henry V,* I. ii). To all orders as way of life there is "fixed as an aim or butt/ Obedience"—as the Arch-bishop goes on to say, using bees as ideals or exempla. (The whole speech is very serious; whatever Stratford producers may choose to do with comic clergymen.) From the principle of Obedience—which really means a complete system of proper respects towards all superiors from parents upwards—it follows that the rightful King is, as it were, the organic nucleus of the cell-State; and that without due and rightful suc-cession all Order (all its vital processes) is put in jeopardy. The only right way with a bad King is non-resistance: biding God's good time in

Christian patience—as Gaunt tells the wronged Duchess of Gloucester—for ill Kings are as much ordained by God as good ones.

The curse of usurpation is that it confuses Right, endangers all Order. That of rebellion is that it commits the Luciferian sin of pride, and destroys all Order: by the assumed "law" that men who will revolt against the highest loyalty (to God's Deputy) cannot be bound by any other loyalty, nor decency. The rebel abrogates all respects; and since the King-enucleated State is ordained by God, by Natural Law, therefore he is a thing *unnatural:* a boil, a plague-sore, a carbuncle of corrupted blood.

This system of notions, with its hysterical terror of treason, is alien to our minds. We can see why the Tudors wanted England convinced that no worse chaos than the Roses civil war had ever come upon the English; especially in the late 1590s, when the Queen was old and had been flattered too much and too long on her immortality to be at all inclined to contemplate her own mortality and fix on her successor. We can see that Shakespeare has this nexus of thought in an astonishing intensity: especially over his horror of the mob — as a hydra-headed incarnation of disorder. I still feel the need of an approach less Tudor-moral. I find it in a MS. note of Coleridge's: "What a world of Love and Bee-like Loyalty and Heart-adherence did the Stuarts trick and tyrannize away."[1]

If we think of the ideal State as bound together like that, by happily unquestioning devotions, we come much nearer at the "politics" of the Histories than by making them rigid, frigidly-patterned Moralities of State-right and State-wrong. (Like Halle, or the Homilies.)

There is real danger of that simplification; and one important ill-effect is on Falstaff. The Dover Wilson Sir John Paunch is dangerously near usurping the place of a much greater man: because any ideological view which makes *Henry IV* into a princely morality reduces Falstaff to little more than a symbol of all the fat and idle temptations which royalty rejects. . . . Already semi-deflated Falstaffs are reaching the stage—Welfare-State Falstaffs, shrunk in the moral wash, or preconditioned for pricking before they have got so far afoot as Shrewsbury. That is not only sad. The effect is to neglect all the comic criticism which Falstaff himself supplies; and also all the complexities of the Henry IV plays, which often result from the use of comic parallelism of phrase or incident. That is, of parody, critically used; or of travesty-by-parallel.

Parody of this kind operates by juxtapositions of opposites; by contrasts so extreme as to seem irreconcilable. In this sense Falstaff at Shrewsbury is a "parody" of knighthood: everything a knight in battle ought *not* to be; that is, IF men are all that theoretical codes assume. . . . It is this travesty-by-parallel which makes Sir John more than a bigger

[1] K. Coburn: *Inquiring Spirit*, p. 249.

and a greater Bluntschli, in this other inquiry into *Arms and the Man:* as much greater as sherris sack is finer, nimbler, more forgetive than chocolate-creams. Parody is used again when Hotspur and Lady Percy have appeared in Act ii. sc. iii., with Hotspur taking an easy leap out of Kate's bed to pluck bright Honour (in a traitorous conspiracy), and rudely ignoring her questions. He calls a servant, asks about a horse— a roan, a crop-ear was it not?—and then pretends he has forgotten all her inquiries. In the next scene, in Eastcheap, the Prince suddenly thinks of Hotspur. What follows?—An exact parallel, a travesty of the Percy *ménage;* and in dialogue, too:

> I am not yet of Percy's mind, the Hotspur of the north; he that kills me some six or seven dozen of Scots at a breakfast, washes his hands, and says to his wife, "Fie upon this quiet life. I want work." "O my sweet Harry," says she, "how many hast thou kill'd today?" "Give my roan horse a drench," says he; and answers "Some fourteen," an hour after, "A trifle, a trifle."

The parallelism is manifest. The next sentence reminds us how farcical travesty *by play-acting* is an intrinsic part of the Eastcheap critique. The Prince continues thus: "I prithee, call in Falstaff. I'll play Percy, and that damned brawn shall play Dame Mortimer his wife. . . ."

It would be merely a mistake to attach this bit of parody to the "character" of Prince Hal and only that; it is a quality of the play. As you can see from the scene at Bangor (iii. i.), where it is *Hotspur* who is the plain-man parodist—of the fantastic Welsh-nationalism and supernaturalism of Glendower. Again (I cannot discuss it in detail)—there is the recurrent theme of Falstaff's bogus repentances: all in a play framed on the crude subject of a wild and prodigal Prince's unlikely reformation. The best is in the opening speeches of Act iii. iii.; which follow immediately on the moving and earnest scene of the Prince's vows to repent and reform—the scene with his father. The switch to Falstaff telling Bardolph, "I'll repent and that suddenly, while I am in some liking" (and so on) is another sign of how comic parallelism is thematic in the entire play. I shall next explain my term "Ambivalence" in my own way, and then return to these items, to argue whether these . . . switches are tricks, or mere farce, or something more significant.

AMBIVALENCE

It is hard to persuade everyone that what is laughable may also be serious; or that a man who laughs at something is "thinking" or "as good as thinking" (and maybe better). That is, unless it is when a satirist laughs at things we delight in or revere; then we call it "mocking" and say he's a horrid fellow.

That is what I mean by "Ambivalence": that two opposed value-judgements are subsumed, and that both are valid (i.e. for that work of art or the mind producing it). The whole is only fully experienced when both opposites are held and included in a "two-eyed" view; and all "one-eyed" simplifications are not only falsifications; they amount to a denial of some part of the mystery of things.

Return now to Shakespeare. I can do no more but only remark in passing how irony—including "dramatic irony"—is a display of an essential ambivalence. Dramatic irony causes an exact juxtaposition of opposites in the mind of the audience: opposites, in that the "true" for one hearer (the stage Persona) must exclude the "true" for other hearers, who take the same words in a far extended sense, of which the hearing Persona is known to be unaware. ("Fail not our feast," e.g.) Yet both meanings only happen in the same mind: the audience's or reader's. The emotive effect is a terrifying belittlement of human prescience or judgement, as in tragedy, when we project the simple meaning on to the mind of a Macbeth, then contemplate it, as it were, against the ironized, unsimple meaning. Or, where sympathy lacks, the effect is some kind of detached sardonic amusement: as in some of Richard III's ironies, or, perhaps, in watching Falstaff and Co. scampering up to London for Harry's coronation, with Shallow in tow and all to the tune of: "Let us take any man's horses. The laws of England are at my commandment. Happy are they which have been my friends; and woe unto my Lord Chief Justice."

We have seen the Prince reconciled to the L.C.J.—we know the rest. But though this is still irony, it is now Comic Irony: in which pathos, derision, a sad wry smile and a malicious grin strive together—and all "belong." A modern Mirror-for-Magistrates view, to which Falstaff is only the "Vice" to be formally discarded in a moral interlude of princely education, leaves just nothing of all that doubleness of feeling.

But Shakespearian History plays double tunes on far more than the comic aspects of the misfortunes of an old fat cynical reprobate—even when they do (as here) symbolize the absurd vanity of human wishings (which supply all beggars with dream-horses at the twinkle of a main-chance). Consider how in both parts of *Henry IV* the shady and seamy sides of glorious War are presented; and comically. In Part 1 Falstaff explains how he damnably misuses the King's press (Act IV. sc. ii.). In Part 2 a full-length exposition of the game is given (in III. ii.), with Feeble as the unwittingly ironical commentator—laughed at for a fool, yet the only man's-size voice in Gloucestershire:

By my troth, I care not; a man can die but once; we owe God a death. I'll ne'er bear a base mind. An't be my destiny, so; an't be not, so. No man's too good to serve's Prince . . .

The Mug is the Hero, without prejudice to his mug-dom: the Fool is the only clear-seer. Ambivalence again. And all comic; though implicitly all these "King's press" episodes are serious commentary on the wickedness and irresponsibility inseparable from WAR. Damnably wrong, clean contrary to all the war-values associated with Crécy, Agincourt or Harfleur . . . and *therefore* a critical comic commentary on a set of human facts which the "Agincourt-values" insist on viewing (if at all) with one eye only. "Two voices are there," as Wordsworth said in quite another connection: "This is damnably wicked," says the one. "It's damn' funny," says the other. Historian Shakespeare heard both.

I shall not labour to explain how the famous "Honour" catechism comically balances the accounts of that main term in *1 Henry IV;* but I must remark on the beautifully complicated parallelisms generated when Falstaff tells the Prince how his father has sent for him, and that he had best rehearse before he goes to the palace to explain himself. It is a scene which travesty-parallels the true meeting later (in III. ii), and it is Eastcheap interlude-acting played to the height.

First, KING Falstaff rebukes his "son" (with a parody of Puritan oratory), allowing that he *has* observed *one* virtuous man in Harry's company: "If that man should be lewdly given, he deceiveth me; for, Harry, I see virtue in his looks." Next, the Prince insists that they change roles, and we have the Prince (as King) pretending just what he will *have* to pretend when he *is* King: viz. that Falstaff is "an old white-bearded Satan," a "villainous misleader of youth." The picture is the obverse of Falstaff's; but now Shakespeare goes one better still, and makes Falstaff as Prince offer a final turn of defence—ending with "Banish not him thy Harry's company. . . . Banish plump Jack, and banish all the world." To which the King-Prince replies—as the Prince-King will have to in earnest—"I do, I will."

In that three-move epitome you have all the special technique of the *Henry IV* plays: a constant shifting of appearances, like the changing lights of an opal, so that every event, every person becomes equivocal—as Falstaff made Honour. That Gadshill robbery is not mere farce. If we "realize" it, in an Usurper's state where Henry's right is only that of might, might only—then what are the Percies and Bolingbrokes but Gadshills, Bardolphs, Petos in Bigger Business?

> Thieves for their robbery have authority
> When judges steal themselves,

so says Isabella in *Measure for Measure.* The comic robbing of the robbers is comically parallel to what the King would do with Percy's Scots prisoners; and the difficulty of establishing the Right in anything, in an England under no rightful king, is paralleled and parodied throughout in Falstaff's "manner of wrenching the true cause the false way"—whether in the inventive proliferation of buckram men, in belying Mrs. Quickly to the Lord Chief Justice, or bamboozling her into vigorous denials of her own (perhaps not impeccable) virtue. I mean where he calls her an otter, and explains "She's neither fish nor flesh; a man knows not where to have her." To which the wronged woman replies in great moral indignation, "Thou art an unjust man in saying so. Thou or any man knows where to have me, thou knave thou."

It is in all such places—in Falstaff as the Wit: the witty equivocator who turns all to mirth, destroying ideals and seriousnesses with a turn of the word—that the Comic Histories go beyond anything that Shakespeare attempted in *Richard II*. There, too, that the narrowly Tudor-political or "moral" approach will most oversimplify, and thin, the true Shakespearian vintage. The "moral-historical" approach diminishes Falstaff as Wit, leaving him with little more than the rascally quick-wittedness which gets Eulenspiegels and Harlequins out of tight corners. Sir John is more. He is not only witty in himself . . . he is Wit ipse. And wit is critically destructive—of ideal systems which assume that human nature is what it isn't. The doubleness of implicit values in those situations which are ambivalent; those which can be seen as serious *and* farcical: as pathetic *and* absurd: as abominable *and* laughable: as fine-and-admirable *and* as all-very-fine-and-large; all that centres on Falstaff. To read it as simply "evil" (or "the antithesis of the Princely virtues") and to make "evil" the opposite of the Order required by the military State of a Henry V, is too naïve. And I don't mean just "too naïve for 1951," I mean "Too naïve for the mind of a Shakespeare, in 1599." As Walter Raleigh wrote:

> This is indeed the everlasting difficulty of Shakespeare criticism, that the critics are so much more moral than Shakespeare himself, and so much less experienced. . . . The ready judgments which are often passed on Shakespeare's most difficult characters are like the talk of children. Childhood is amazingly moral, with a confident, dictatorial, unflinching morality. The work of experience . . . is to undermine this early pedantry . . . to teach tolerance, or at least suspense of judgment.

That's a "period-piece," no doubt, and I wouldn't endorse its rather shapeless liberalism, which half suggests the (to me absurd) conclusion that Shakespeare is not moral at all—let alone one of the greatest of moralists. But Raleigh didn't have the word "doctrinaire" to hand, I suppose. The warning he gives is by no means out of date, I should say.

I hope I'm not slipping towards (what he would call) the surprising moral immaturity of some of our doctrinaire contemporaries, if I say that there is, in Falstaffian wit, something of the devaluating skill of The Devil. Let me hide behind Coleridge to advance my point. In table-talking on 16 February 1833, Coleridge gave a long account of a Faust play he had designed before ever he read Goethe. (I don't believe him, but that's unimportant.) He said, "My Devil was to be, like Goethe's, the Universal Humorist, who should make all things vain and nothing worth, by a perpetual collation of the Great with the Little in the presence of the Infinite." Now surely that is very near to what Falstaff does, when most the Clown critical. "The perpetual collation of the Great with the Little" is no bad formula for what Shakespeare is repeatedly doing in both *Henry IV* plays.

In Part 2, however, the Universal Humorist is a far more sardonic one than before. Not only in that Old Age, in its failings, its brags, its pavidities and follies, is a major theme; nor only that Lord John of Lancaster's "victory" is disgracefully won; there is more besides. . . .

Rumour's prologue offers a theme which runs right through the whole play; a theme which invites a sardonic, detached, unsympathetic or coldly-critical attitude towards all the agents in the historic field. *False-report befools everyone.* Not only in the rumoured rebel victory at Shrewsbury; not only in the false (favourable) report of Falstaff's prowess—to which Coleville surrenders, and which even the L.C.J. makes some allowance for. Falstaff's own trust in the Prince and his star is also "smooth comforts false": as is old Shallow's trust in Sir John and the smell of Court. So too—false—is this same Shallow's roaring-boy Past in London. And Pistol is false-alarm personified: mouthfuls of Theatre masquerading as a man—whereas he is nothing but wind. And thus the parallel to "Sir John to all Europe": the vain delusion to which Coleville surrenders, as the northern rebels surrender to "smooth comforts false" from Westmorland and Prince John. Finally, the King—King Hal the First—that Falstaff expected to find in London is only a delusion; and the laugh is on Falstaff—with a grating edge to the amusement. (A. C. Bradley only encountered this unhappy Mixed Feeling at the Rejection. In fact it starts much earlier in the play. Modern "moral" critics apparently never meet it at all.)

These shifting mirage-like effects of unstable appearances relate Part 2 to the so-called "Problem Plays" (which *I* call "Tragi-comedies"). They develop from, e.g., the Honour theme of Part I, but go well beyond that historical Comedy.

And if you wonder why—talking on The Histories—I say so little about *Richard II* and *Henry V*, my answer is: I am diagnosing their shortcomings by focusing attention on Shakespearian History at its highest development. (I say "History." If you want to see this kind of thing taken on, in later work, go to the Galley-scene in *Antony and Cleopatra*: a similar comedy, sardonic comedy, of the frailty of the Great: the strange absurd chances that turn the fate of worlds.) But in *Richard II* —either Shakespeare was bent on following Marlowe and writing an un-English tragedy (i.e. without comic interplay: though *Woodstock* put it directly before him); or he knew instinctively that the preciosity and self-regarding sentiment of Richard *could not stand* comic criticism or even lapse of seriousness.

In *Henry V* his aim was changed. Whatever he once intended (and that last speech, by the Dancer, in *2 Henry IV*, does show the *intention* to export Falstaff to France), what he produced was a propaganda-play on National Unity: heavily orchestrated for the brass. The sounding— and very impressive—Rhetoric shows how something is being stifled. The wartime-values demand a determined "one-eyedness"; the King fails to reach the fullest humanity because of that demand. He *has* banished Plump Jack; and "all the World" has been banished with him. At least, the "Allness" is gone. The play is "fracted and corroborate."

Without going all the way with "Q," to say that Falstaff must go to "Arthur's bosom" because he can kill Harry with a look, I do agree that Sir John had to be dead; for fear of the damage he must needs have done by babbling of (not "green fields") . . . by killing the heroics with a jest. When the ranks are closed, and to question is to lack Will, to falter, then there is not so much freedom of mind as will say *outright* what every sane man knows (however brave): "I like not such grinning Honour as Sir Walter hath. . . . Give me Life, say I."

There are fine things in *Henry V;* but much of the comedy has lost touch with the serious matter. It's a play Shakespeare had finished with well before he finished it. His falling-back on the old *Famous Victories* for that slapdash stuff—treating the Princess of France like a Free French-woman, etc.—that shows it. It surprises me that our London dramatic critics should have been surprised to find that as a climax to the 1951 Stratford historical tetralogy it does not come off. The truth is, the heart of Shakespeare's insight into English History (which means a good deal more than the History of England)—the *heart* is in the middle of the sequence: in the *Henry IV* plays, where he turned back from the senti-mental seriousness of *Richard II*, back to the kind of Comic History he had made rough beginnings with in Parts 2 and 3 of *Henry VI*. (Where he had achieved something remarkable in the grotesque, Hieronymus-Bosch-like sarcastically-comic scenes of Cade's rebellion.) [2]

To see why *comic* History was his true genre, it is needless to go back to the evolution of the Elizabethan Drama and its Miracle-play and Morality-play underlays. "Mungrell tragy-comedy" *was* the mere-Eng-lish genre, but never mind that now. Look only at *King John*—those

---

[2] I mean such Bosch paintings as *Ecce Homo* and the Veronica picture, where the mob is not only grotesque—absurd and half-diabolic—but also presents itself as a kind of hydra: *belua capitum multorum;* cf. Rumour's "the blunt monster with uncounted heads," etc. The phrase was a commonplace, unoriginal even in Horace's day; but Bosch actualizes it in paint, as Shakespeare does in drama. A European tradition is shared by the Flemish painters and Shakespeare. I explored a fringe of it in an article on *Breugel's Ambivalences* in *The Cambridge Journal* for December 1948.

lines by the Bastard on "Commodity" ("Mad world, mad kings . . . etc.")
—and you will see how they take the gilded lid off the lofty illusions of
theoretical Tudor Politics (I mean *Stage*-politics). By-passing all the
ideals of Order, Degree, Non-resistance, Right-divine and God's-deputy-
ship, the Bastard exposed the world of politics as "a racket."[3] The
thought implicit in the making of that speech has the same quality of
deep political penetration that emerges from the conflict of serious and
comic in *Henry IV*—and in *Coriolanus* and *Antony and Cleopatra.* That
speech shows the same ambivalence, but simpler; for Falconbridge is a
noble fighting humorist as well as a critical wit. He is not, like Falstaff,
a Universal Humorist; but some of the undermining intellectual clear-
sightedness of the later Histories is there.

Throughout the Histories it is in the implications of the Comic that
shrewd, realistic thinking about men in politics—in office—in war—in plot
—is exposed: realistic apprehension outrunning the medieval frame. Because the Tudor myth system of Order, Degree, etc. was too rigid, too
black-and-white, too doctrinaire and narrowly moral for Shakespeare's
mind: it falsified his fuller experience of men. Consequently, while
employing it as FRAME, he had to undermine it, to qualify it with equivo-
cations: to vex its applications with sly or subtle ambiguities: to cast
doubts on its ultimate human validity, even in situations where its principles seemed most completely applicable. His intuition told him it was
morally inadequate.

Hence the unhappy feelings which generous-minded critics have dis-
played about the Rejection of Falstaff. That some of them have *over-
done* it is neither here nor there. It is well enough for Dr. Tillyard or
Professor Dover Wilson to tell us that the Prince *had* to cast off Sir John.
We know that. We know what Kingship meant to textbook Tudors (far
better than the Globe audiences knew, I dare say). Yet I still feel that
as Shakespeare *was* Shakespeare—the man who made Hermione and
Hamlet, drew Kate Percy as war-widow (a traitor's wife by the Code),
drew Katherine as the fallen majesty of England—he must have known,
and felt, the lack of humanity (of generosity, high-mindedness, true
magnanimity) in his Hal in that scene. And again, I think, in Henry's
treatment of the conspirators at Southampton; where the King is so
obviously playing a publicity propaganda part, as Justice, iron-visaged,
pitiless. . . . As obviously as he said he was in that first of unprincely
soliloquies, "I know you all. . . " (*1 Henry IV*, I. ii. end.)

Is there not a resemblant quality in his father: the "silent king,"

[3] This was put too crudely. I would add now: Shakespeare wrote in an unstable equilibrium between a "World" or "Universe-of-thought" of faith in God-ordainedness, and another World: the Inverted World of belief only in Power. The "Inverted World" symbol
is familiar in Breugel's pictures, as an orb with its cross downwards. The "upsidedown-
ness" notion is in *Measure for Measure* and elsewhere. The pictorial emblem itself appears
in Quarles (e.g. *Emblems* i. 15).

Bolingbroke, in the mirror-episode in *Richard II?* A separateness from
the feeling world, which makes the actor in public affairs assume a pre-
determined part, like a *play-actor,* only with all his directives outside
and none of his? One of those "who, moving others, are themselves as
stone," as the sonnet phrases it: "the lords and owners of their faces"?
And thus again a resemblant quality in John of Lancaster's treachery to
the northern rebels? Oh, I know it can be argued that, to the Elizabethans, no ill treatment or trickery towards rebels could be unjustified.
But can we assume that Shakespeare's sensibilities were so crass as not
to know meanness as meanness, perfidy as perfidy, when it could be said
to have profited the State? I say no more than, "I think not." And if you
agree on any of these points I've hung on to the Rejection of Falstaff,
doesn't it follow that you are made to *feel* (not merely "see," notionally)
how the frame of Order, the coherent rigid medieval system accepted by
some of our most reputed modern scholars, is outrun by that mind which
Jonson (who "knew the man . . . etc.") considered to be "not for an age
but for all time"?

It follows, if I have taken you along with me, that we cannot dissect-
out, stain and fix the system of Shakespeare's reflexion on History. A
rigid political-moral good-and-evil system is there; but as the events and
the people speak into our inner mind, we find that Shakespeare is shifting subtly from key to key, as if by what musicians call "enharmonic
changes": using ambiguous note-sequences till contradiction is itself
confounded, and yields a precise evocation of the paradox of human
experience.

Thomas Mann has explored this musical symbolism to the limit in his
vast, amazing, fascinatingly wearisome novel *Doktor Faustus.* When his
damned musical genius, Adrian Leverkühn, makes his first experiments
with notes, the narrator (Serenus Zeitblom Ph.D.) records a comment
which seems to be saying a lot about what I find in the ambivalences of
Shakespeare. "Relationship is everything," said Leverkühn. "And if you
want to give it a more precise name, it is Ambiguity . . ." And again,
later, "You know what I find?—That music turns the equivocal into a
system" (pp. 47 f. of the American translation approved by Mann.
Knopf, 1947).

What is more, Leverkühn finds something amenable to his music in
Shakespeare. He takes *Love's Labour's Lost* as a theme to treat. On
this Zeitblom reports, "He spoke with enthusiasm of the theme, which
gave opportunity to set the lout and the "natural" alongside the comic
sublime, and make both ridiculous in each other." Mann is not explicit,
but it is clear enough that he means the three lover-nobles by "comic
sublime," placed *vis-à-vis* Costard as "the natural." Zeitblom Ph.D. is
unhappy about it: "I have always been rather unhappy at the mockery
of humanistic extravagances; it ends by making Humanism itself a sub-

ject for mirth" (p. 164). That would be a good text for setting out to explore the entire subject of so-called "Comic Relief" in Shakespeare. I must keep within my limits, come back to Histories.

"Music turns the equivocal into a system." That is why I used the phrase "The Dialectic of the Histories" in my—admittedly alarming— title (for which I now apologize). The Order-code-system of Tudor theory approaches History with the kind of argument that Plato called *eristic:* that is, argument aimed at the extinction of an opposite and "bad" system of beliefs. The code is moral, but in the narrow sense: too much so for Shakespeare's contemplation of mankind; too narrow and bounded for his human insight, from which he derived a *political* wisdom. As Hazlitt once observed:

> Shakespeare was in one sense the least moral of all writers; for morality (commonly so called) is made up of antipathies; and his talent consisted in sympathy with human nature in all its shapes, degrees, depressions and elevations.

I shan't examine that for its shortcomings, beyond saying that it is *morally* acuter than Raleigh—as witness the distinction "morality commonly so called." Taking it as it stands, then, I say: Therefore, Shakespeare's intuitive way of thinking about History (which we cannot formulate as an abstracted notional system) is *dialectical*. The old eristic-argumentative system which he used is static, changeless; but *his* thought is dynamic, alterative, not tied to its age. It has that extra degree-of-freedom which is given only by what I called a constant "Doubleness": a thoroughly English empiricism which recognizes the coextancy and juxtaposition of opposites, without submitting to urges (philosophical, moral, etc.) to obliterate or annihilate the one in the theoretic interests of the other. That is what I tried to express by the figure of "two-eyedness."

His awareness of the "soul of goodness in things evil" is not less than his sense of the spirit of seriousness (or significance) in things base—or foolish—or farcical—or indecent. To laugh at Hotspurious honour is as good as to think. To laugh at Shallow, or at Falstaff with Doll Tearsheet, is the substance of some wry or wringing thinking. But no less funny for that. And thus it is that the serio-comic dialectic of the Histories leads on to the Tragedies, where you have (as in the Histories you have not, I consider) Coleridge's "collation of the Great and the Little *in the presence of the Infinite*." In none of the Tragedies is the Order-system the friend of human greatness; rather the enemy.

If you have difficulty in refusing the critics' directions to see Henry V as Shakespeare's Ideal; if you cannot quite accept what I've said about the constant Doubleness of the Shakespearian vision in the Histories; then let me ask you to face a straight question: "Who, in the later, greater plays, are the heirs and successors of those Order-symbols Henry V and Henry Tudor (the triumphant Richmond of the end of *Richard III*)? The men who are, to the State-order system, 'goods': unifying nuclei of the organism, whether a People or the mind itself: the beings on whom the political heaven smiles. Who are they?" I should reply, "The Fortinbrasses, the Octavii, Lodovicos, Macduffs, the Edgars and Albanies. On whose heroic qualities Bradley is, for once, entirely adequate."

But why is "the other side," the reverse to the kingly, historic, patriotic obverse, the Comic? Is it not partly this? In History Shakespeare felt that men were constrained to be much less than their full selves. He knew the burden of princehood: the Ceremony lines alone would proclaim it. All the Lancasters are less than full men. None is himself; only what he wills to be for the time only. By and by he will "be more himself." Hal says it: Father says it. None does it. Richard does try to be himself, full kingly length. He finds a shadow in a mirror. Only the other Richard—Gloucester—can say, "I am myself alone." And *he* is the Devil, spinning the orb on his thumb. Now Comedy is the field of human shortcoming; and therefore Shakespeare's History, at its greatest, *had* to be comic. What isn't Comic History in the Histories is what I can only call "Obscure tragedy."

At the very end of his career, back here at New Place, collaborating with young bright immoral John Fletcher in his last history-play (or so I think; and others more eminent do not)—he brought the same elements into *Henry VIII*. The man of forty-eight had not changed his mind. That was 1612; in 1616 he was dead. I hope that he was ending in something like the mind of those lines of Yeats:

> No longer in Lethean foliage caught
> Begin the preparation for your death
> And from the fortieth winter by that thought
> Test every work of intellect or faith,
> And everything that your own hands have wrought;
> And call those works extravagance of breath
> That are not suited for such men as come
> Proud, open-eyed, and laughing to the tomb.

Note. In preparing this lecture for print, I have made no attempt to convert it to a literary "essay," nor, indeed, to do more than fill in the breaks and gaps of my lecture-notes with words to the same effect as those I used at the time. Similarly, with only one or two exceptions (mere topical asides) I have left in those parenthetical turns which a speaking voice can make much easier for hearers than they usually are for a reader. The style of the whole was intended for public delivery, and in my own manner of lecturing. To print it as anything other than a very close transcript of the actual lecture would have meant a complete rewriting; and for that I had neither the leisure nor the taste.—A.P.R.

SAMUEL TAYLOR COLERIDGE

Richard II and the Character of the King

THE TRANSITIONAL STATE between the epic and the drama is the historic drama. In the epic a pre-announced fate gradually adjusts and employs the will and the incidents as its instruments (*'ἕπομαι, sequor*), while the drama places fate and will in opposition [and is] then most perfect when the victory of fate is obtained in consequence of imperfections in the opposing will, so as to leave the final impression that the fate itself is but a higher and more intelligent Will.

From the length of the speeches, the number of long speeches, and that (with one exception) the events are all *historical,* presented in their *results,* not produced by acts seen, or that take place before the audience, this tragedy is ill-suited to our present large theatres. But in itself, and for the closet, I feel no hesitation in placing it the first and most admirable of all Shakespeare's *purely* historical plays. For the two parts of *Henry IV.* form a species of themselves, which may be named the *mixt drama.* The distinction does not depend on the quantity of historical events compared with the fictions, for there is as much *history* in *Macbeth* as in *Richard,* but in the relation of the history to the plot. In the purely historical plays, the history *informs* the plot; in the mixt it *directs* it; in the rest, as *Macbeth, Hamlet, Cymbeline, Lear,* it subserves it.

But this Richard II. O God forbid that however unsuited for the stage yet even there it should fall dead on the hearts of jacobinized Englishmen. Then indeed *praeteriit gloria mundi.* The spirit of patriotic reminiscence is the all-permeating spirit of this drama. . . .

I. iv. A striking conclusion of a first act—letting the reader into the secret [of Richard's weakness], having before impressed the dignified and kingly manners of Richard, yet by well managed anticipations

From *Coleridge's Shakespearean Criticism,* ed. T. M. Raysor (Cambridge, Mass., 1930), vol. I, pp. 142–143, 148–149; vol. II, pp. 186–188. Published by E. P. Dutton & Co. Reprinted by permission of Professor Raysor. Also by permission of J. M. Dent & Sons, Ltd. Footnotes from that edition have been omitted. Title supplied by the present editor. The passages have been abridged.

leading to the full gratification of the auditor's pleasure in his own penetration.

In this scene a new light is thrown on Richard's character. Until now he has appeared in all the beauty of royalty; but here, as soon as he is left to himself, the inherent weakness of his character is immediately shown. It is a weakness, however, of a peculiar kind, not arising from want of personal courage, or any specific defect of faculty, but rather an intellectual feminineness which feels a necessity of ever leaning on the breast of others, and of reclining on those who are all the while known to be inferiors. To this must be attributed as its consequences all Richard's vices, his tendency to concealment, and his cunning, the whole operation of which is directed to the getting rid of present difficulties. Richard is not meant to be a debauchee; but we see in him that sophistry which is common to man, by which we can deceive our own hearts, and at one and the same time apologize for, and yet commit, the error. Shakespeare has represented this character in a very peculiar manner. He has not made him amiable with counterbalancing faults; but has openly and broadly drawn those faults without reserve, relying on Richard's disproportionate sufferings and gradually emergent good qualities for our sympathy; and this was possible, because his faults are not positive vices, but spring entirely from defect of character.

[II. i. 84. Gaunt's punning on his death-bed.
K. Rich. Can sick men play so nicely with their names?]

The passion that carries off its excess by play on words, as naturally and, therefore, as appropriately to drama, as by gesticulations, looks, or tones. . . .

In order to decide this point, it is obviously necessary to consider the state of mind, and the degree of passion, of the person using this play upon words. Resort to this grace may, in some cases, deserve censure, not because it is a play upon words, but because it is a play upon words in a wrong place, and at a wrong time. What is right in one state of mind is wrong in another, and much more depends upon that, than upon the conceit (so to call it) itself. I feel the importance of these remarks strongly, because the greater part of the abuse, I might say filth, thrown out and heaped upon Shakespeare, has originated in want of consideration. Dr. Johnson asserts that Shakespeare loses the world for a toy, and can no more withstand a pun, or a play upon words, than his Antony could resist Cleopatra. Certain it is, that Shakespeare gained more admiration in his day, and long afterwards, by the use of speech in this way, than modern writers have acquired by the abandonment of the practice: the latter, in adhering to, what they have been pleased to call, the rules of art, have sacrificed nature.

Having said thus much on the, often falsely supposed, blemishes of

our poet—blemishes which are said to prevail in "Richard II." especially,
—I will now advert to the character of the King. He is represented as a
man not deficient in immediate courage, which displays itself at his
assassination; or in powers of mind, as appears by the foresight he exhibits throughout the play: still, he is weak, variable, and womanish,
and possesses feelings, which, amiable in a female, are misplaced in a
man, and altogether unfit for a king. In prosperity he is insolent and
presumptuous, and in adversity, if we are to believe Dr. Johnson, he is
humane and pious. I cannot admit the latter epithet, because I perceive
the utmost consistency of character in Richard: what he was at first,
he is at last, excepting as far as he yields to circumstances: what he
shewed himself at the commencement of the play, he shews himself at
the end of it. Dr. Johnson assigns to him rather the virtue of a confessor
than that of a king.

True it is, that he may be said to be overwhelmed by the earliest misfortune that befalls him; but, so far from his feelings or disposition
being changed or subdued, the very first glimpse of the returning sun-
shine of hope reanimates his spirits, and exalts him to as strange and
unbecoming a degree of elevation, as he was before sunk in mental
depression: the mention of those in his misfortunes, who had contributed
to his downfall, but who had before been his nearest friends and favour-
ites, calls forth from him expressions of the bitterest hatred and revenge.
Thus, where Richard asks:

> Where is the Earl of Wiltshire? Where is Bagot?
> What is become of Bushy? Where is Green?
> That they have let the dangerous enemy
> Measure our confines with such peaceful steps?
> If we prevail, their heads shall pay for it.
> I warrant they have made peace with Bolingbroke.
> *Act III., Scene 2.*

Scroop answers:

> Peace have they made with him, indeed, my lord.

Upon which Richard, without hearing more, breaks out:

> O villains! vipers, damn'd without redemption!
> Dogs, easily won to fawn on any man!
> Snakes, in my heart-blood warm'd, that sting my heart!
> Three Judases, each one thrice worse than Judas!
> Would they make peace? terrible hell make war
> Upon their spotted souls for this offence!

Scroop observes upon this change, and tells the King how they had
made their peace:

> Sweet love, I see, changing his property
> Turns to the sourest and most deadly hate.
> Again uncurse their souls: their peace is made
> With heads and not with hands: those whom you curse
> Have felt the worst of death's destroying wound,
> And lie full low, grav'd in the hollow ground.

Richard receiving at first an equivocal answer,—"Peace have they made with him, indeed, my lord,"—takes it in the worst sense: his promptness to suspect those who had been his friends turns his love to hate, and calls forth the most tremendous execrations.

From the beginning to the end of the play he pours out all the peculiarities and powers of his mind: he catches at new hope, and seeks new friends, is disappointed, despairs, and at length makes a merit of his resignation. He scatters himself into a multitude of images, and in conclusion endeavours to shelter himself from that which is around him by a cloud of his own thoughts. Throughout his whole career may be noticed the most rapid transitions—from the highest insolence to the lowest humility—from hope to despair, from the extravagance of love to the agonies of resentment, and from pretended resignation to the bitterest reproaches. The whole is joined with the utmost richness and copiousness of thought, and were there an actor capable of representing Richard, the part would delight us more than any other of Shakespeare's master-pieces,—with, perhaps, the single exception of King Lear. I know of no character drawn by our great poet with such unequalled skill as that of Richard II. . . .

WILLIAM BUTLER YEATS

Richard II and Henry V

III

. . . I have turned over many books in the library at Stratford-on-Avon, and I have found in nearly all an antithesis, which grew in clearness and violence as the century grew older, between two types, whose representatives were Richard II., "sentimental," "weak," "selfish," "insincere," and Henry V., "Shakespeare's only hero." These books took the same delight in abasing Richard II. that school-boys do in persecuting some boy of fine temperament, who has weak muscles and a distaste for school games. And they had the admiration for Henry V. that school-boys have for the sailor or soldier hero of a romance in some boys' paper. I cannot claim any minute knowledge of these books, but I think that these emotions began among the German critics, who perhaps saw something French and Latin in Richard II., and I know that Professor Dowden, whose book I once read carefully, first made these emotions eloquent and plausible. He lived in Ireland, where everything has failed, and he meditated frequently upon the perfection of character which had, he thought, made England successful, for, as we say, "cows beyond the water have long horns." He forgot that England, as Gordon has said, was made by her adventurers, by her people of wildness and imagination and eccentricity; and thought that Henry V., who only seemed to be these things because he had some commonplace vices, was not only the typical Anglo-Saxon, but the model Shakespeare held up before England; and he even thought it worth while pointing out that Shakespeare himself was making a large fortune while he was writing about Henry's victories. In Professor Dowden's successors this apotheosis went further; and it reached its height at a moment of imperialistic enthusiasm, of ever-deepening conviction that the commonplace shall inherit the earth, when somebody of reputation, whose name I cannot remem-

Reprinted with permission of The Macmillan Company from *Essays and Introductions* by William Butler Yeats pp. 108–114. Copyright 1961 by Mrs. W. B. Yeats. Title supplied by the present editor.

ber, wrote that Shakespeare admired this one character alone out of all his characters. The Accusation of Sin produced its necessary fruit, hatred of all that was abundant, extravagant, exuberant, of all that sets a sail for shipwreck, and flattery of the commonplace emotions and conventional ideals of the mob, the chief Paymaster of accusation.

IV

I cannot believe that Shakespeare looked on his Richard II. with any but sympathetic eyes, understanding indeed how ill-fitted he was to be King, at a certain moment of history, but understanding that he was lovable and full of capricious fancy, "a wild creature" as Pater has called him. The man on whom Shakespeare modelled him had been full of French elegancies, as he knew from Holinshed, and had given life a new luxury, a new splendour, and been "too friendly" to his friends, "too favourable" to his enemies. And certainly Shakespeare had these things in his head when he made his King fail, a little because he lacked some qualities that were doubtless common among his scullions, but more because he had certain qualities that are uncommon in all ages. To suppose that Shakespeare preferred the men who deposed his King is to suppose that Shakespeare judged men with the eyes of a Municipal Councillor weighing the merits of a Town Clerk; and that had he been by when Verlaine cried out from his bed, "Sir you have been made by the stroke of a pen, but I have been made by the breath of God," he would have thought the Hospital Superintendent the better man. He saw indeed, as I think, in Richard II. the defeat that awaits all, whether they be Artist or Saint, who find themselves where men ask of them a rough energy and have nothing to give but some contemplative virtue, whether lyrical phantasy, or sweetness of temper, or dreamy dignity, or love of God, or love of His creatures. He saw that such a man through sheer bewilderment and impatience can become as unjust or as violent as any common man, any Bolingbroke or Prince John, and yet remain "that sweet lovely rose." The courtly and saintly ideals of the Middle Ages were fading, and the practical ideals of the modern age had begun to threaten the unuseful dome of the sky; Merry England was fading, and yet it was not so faded that the Poets could not watch the procession of the world with that untroubled sympathy for men as they are, as apart from all they do and seem, which is the substance of tragic irony.

Shakespeare cared little for the State, the source of all our judgments, apart from its shows and splendours, its turmoils and battles, its flamings out of the uncivilized heart. He did indeed think it wrong to overturn a King, and thereby to swamp peace in civil war, and the historical plays from *Henry IV.* to *Richard III.*, that monstrous birth and last sign

of the wrath of Heaven, are a fulfilment of the prophecy of the Bishop
of Carlisle, who was "raised up by God" to make it; but he had no nice
sense of utilities, no ready balance to measure deeds, like that fine
instrument, with all the latest improvements, Gervinus and Professor
Dowden handle so skilfully. He meditated as Solomon, not as Bentham
meditated, upon blind ambitions, untoward accidents, and capricious
passions, and the world was almost as empty in his eyes as it must be
in the eyes of God.

> Tired with all these, for restful death I cry;—
>   As, to behold desert a beggar born,
> And needy nothing trimm'd in jollity,
>   And purest faith unhappily forsworn,
> And gilded honour shamefully misplaced,
>   And maiden virtue rudely strumpeted,
> And right perfection wrongfully disgraced,
>   And strength by limping sway disabled,
> And Art made tongue-tied by authority,
>   And folly, doctor-like, controlling skill,
> And simple truth miscall'd simplicity,
>   And captive good attending captain ill:
> Tired with all these, from these would I be gone,
> Save that, to die, I leave my love alone.

v

The Greeks, a certain scholar has told me, considered that myths are
the activities of the Dæmons, and that the Dæmons shape our characters
and our lives. I have often had the fancy that there is some one Myth
for every man, which, if we but knew it, would make us understand
all he did and thought. Shakespeare's Myth, it may be, describes a wise
man who was blind from very wisdom, and an empty man who thrust
him from his place, and saw all that could be seen from very emptiness.
It is in the story of Hamlet, who saw too great issues everywhere to play
the trivial game of life, and of Fortinbras, who came from fighting battles
about "a little patch of ground" so poor that one of his captains would
not give "six ducats" to "farm it," and who was yet acclaimed by Hamlet
and by all as the only befitting King. And it is in the story of Richard
II., that unripened Hamlet, and of Henry V., that ripened Fortinbras.
To pose character against character was an element in Shakespeare's art,
and scarcely a play is lacking in characters that are the complement of
one another, and so, having made the vessel of porcelain Richard II.,
he had to make the vessel of clay Henry V. He makes him the reverse
of all that Richard was. He has the gross vices, the coarse nerves, of
one who is to rule among violent people, and he is so little "too friendly"
to his friends that he bundles them out of doors when their time is over.

He is as remorseless and undistinguished as some natural force, and the finest thing in his play is the way his old companions fall out of it broken-hearted or on their way to the gallows; and instead of that lyricism which rose out of Richard's mind like the jet of a fountain to fall again where it had risen, instead of that phantasy too enfolded in its own sincerity to make any thought the hour had need of, Shakespeare has given him a resounding rhetoric that moves men, as a leading article does to-day. His purposes are so intelligible to everybody that everybody talks of him as if he succeeded, although he fails in the end, as all men great and little fail in Shakespeare, and yet his conquests abroad are made nothing by a woman turned warrior, and that boy he and Katherine were to "compound," "half French, half English," "that" was to "go to Constantinople and take the Turk by the beard," turns out a Saint and loses all his father had built up at home and his own life.

Shakespeare watched Henry V. not indeed as he watched the greater souls in the visionary procession, but cheerfully, as one watches some handsome spirited horse, and he spoke his tale, as he spoke all tales, with tragic irony.

VI

The five plays, that are but one play, have, when played one after another, something extravagant and superhuman, something almost mythological. These nobles with their indifference to death and their immense energy seem at times no nearer the common stature of men than do the Gods and the heroes of Greek plays. . . .

R. J. DORIUS

Prudence and Excess
in Richard II and the Histories

By showing us the power and frailty of seven kings, Shakespeare's nine English history plays (excluding *Henry VIII*) imply a standard of good kingship which no one of his kings, except possibly Henry V, fully attains. Both this standard and Henry's relationship to it have puzzled many commentators, and with good reason, since the great tragedies imply somewhat different standards, with far more emphasis upon heroic action. The tragic hero's willingness to take terrible risks, to throw away power and life itself for a cause, is not demanded of the kings of the histories. By and large, except for Richard III, they are more conservative; their mission is less to question and dare than to reconcile and maintain. They are absorbed less with the state of man than with practical politics; their problem is not why but how. It follows that they cannot risk the "tragic waste" precipitated by the inflexible highminded resolve of the heroes. Indeed, the overweening ambition of a partly tragic character like Hotspur is seen in the context of the histories as slightly comic.

What seems to set off the values of these plays most markedly from those of the tragedies is the importance given by the histories to the virtues of prudence and economy. For in the chronicle plays these are the essential qualities, together with strength of character—kingliness—for a ruler's governance both of himself and his realm. To what degree the importance of these qualities in Shakespeare, up to the turn of the century, is related to the poet's response to crises of his own day, or to the spectacle of an older England wasted for a hundred years through the incompetence or violence of a succession of weaklings, usurpers, and tyrants, it is difficult to say. But it is clear that the fullest exploration of the significance of prudence and economy in state affairs, and thus

From *Shakespeare Quarterly*, XI (Winter, 1960), 13–26. Reprinted by permission of The Shakespeare Association of America, Inc. First published under the title "A Little More than a Little."

also of their opposites—carelessness, excess, waste, and disease, is to be found in the sequence running from *Richard II* through *Henry V*. It is with the development of these themes of good husbandry and extravagance through the metaphoric language of this tetralogy, and especially of *Richard II*, that this paper will be chiefly concerned. The thematic imagery of these plays possesses a logic and coherence striking enough to justify numerous comparisons between images of different dramas and the assumption that the group forms, in essential features, if not perhaps in initial conception or over-all effect, a unified design.

From Richard's "I wasted time, and now doth time waste me" at the beginning of the series to Henry V's weighing time "Even to the utmost grain" at the end, a concept of good husbandry presides like a goddess over the turbulent experiences of these plays. The assumption behind this emphasis upon watchful economy seems to be that life and power are precious gifts and that to squander them or to misdirect them is a crime against God and the state. And to be careless is to hand one's life and throne over to the initiative of others, who may turn both to their own ends. A negligent and heedless prince, like Richard II, creates a vacuum of power which must be filled, and invites disaster. Throughout, waste or destruction is associated in these plays with an apparently antithetical theme—fatness or excessive growth. Both are the extremes of which economy is the mean, or the ends to which extravagance in man or government might lead. We frequently find in these plays a kind of logical or psychological relationship between the stages of a process from health to disease, marked by metaphors depicting carelessness, eating or sleeping, deafness or blindness, rioting, fatness or excess, sickness, waste, barrenness, and death. The general movement of *Richard II* and of the cycle through *2 Henry IV* is from youthful or springtime luxuriance to aged or wintry barrenness. Of course these polarities are developed more fully in the later Shakespeare. But the well-known association in the great tragedies between images of excess or disease and faults ranging from mere folly to crime is already fully developed in these histories. The significance of Hamlet's dark reference to the world as "an unweeded garden That grows to seed" and to man as a beast whose chief good is "but to sleep and feed" is greatly heightened if seen through the preoccupation with things gross in nature and men in the English histories.

The collaboration of plot, character, and thematic imagery to create a unity of tone and meaning is so intimate in these plays that a word or metaphor can be said to be deepened into character or extended into plot. Thus in *Henry IV* the pervasive imagery of extremes is in a sense embodied both in a lean king of state literally worn away with anxiety and in a fat king of revels surrounded by slivers of himself, "Pharaoh's lean kine." Shape is at least partly an index to character. Everywhere the ideal king, the "figure of God's majesty," is contrasted with the "ugly form Of base and bloody insurrection. . . ."[1] Frequently fast follows feast, early death follows premature growth, in emphatic contrast. In the theatre, the sickness of the divided commonwealth is visibly present in the range of physical proportions of the characters on the stage. In Part II (III. i), the spectacle of the harassed lonely king watching through the night is preceded by the convivial brawling involving fat Saturn and Tearsheet-Venus "in conjunction" and followed by the pricking of the ragamuffins, as Falstaff misuses the king's press. It is almost as though these wastrels, like the crown itself, were, as the Prince says, feeding "upon the body of my father" (IV. v. 160).

The most important antitheses in the histories are often sharpened by what appear to be minor tricks of language. The merry word-games in which the Prince and Falstaff engage, the matchings of "unsavory similes" of fatness and thinness, represent a comic playing with political and moral themes at the core of these plays. One of Falstaff's favorite puns points up the connection between waste and fatness. "Your means are very slender, and your waste is great," says the Chief Justice, posed against Falstaff at the beginning of Part II, and Falstaff replies, "I would my means were greater and my waist slenderer" (I. ii. 160–163). Tagged as Sir John Paunch by Hal, Falstaff rejoins, "Indeed, I am not John of Gaunt, your grandfather . . ." (I:II. ii. 70–71). What begins in a word or name can come to suggest a way of life. One of the polar oppositions to the careless John who sleeps upon benches afternoons and has the "disease of not list'ning" (II:I. ii. 138) is this care-worn John who puns on his own name before Richard II:

> For sleeping England long time have I watch'd;
> Watching breeds leanness, leanness is all gaunt. (II. i. 77–78)

We usually find in the histories that the responsible man and state are thin, the heedless usually fat. Honor-seeking Hotspur, "Amongst a grove the very straightest plant," can be contrasted not only with Falstaff, "out of all order, out of all compass," who reduces honor to a word, but with Richard II, who stoops "with oppression" of the "prodigal weight" of his nobles. Indeed, imagery of over-eating is applied both to the rightful ruler and the usurper, as the sickness of the head of the state develops. From Gaunt's remark about the "eager feeding" which "doth choke the feeder," young Richard (II. i. 37), to Worcester's criticism in *Henry IV* of the lean king who once set out to purge the state of its excesses, is in many ways a single movement. Henry IV, made "portly" by the help of the Percies,

---

[1] References to Part 2 of *Henry IV* are indicated thus: II:IV. i. 39–40. All readings are from the *Complete Works*, edited by G. L. Kittredge, Boston, 1936.

did oppress our nest;
Grew by our feeding to so great a bulk
That even our love durst not come near your sight
For fear of swallowing. . . .   (I:V. i. 61–64)

The eaters are eaten and the would-be physicians become centers of con-
tagion. The lean may wax and the fat wane, but all go to extremes.
Henry IV speaks what might be the motto of the histories: "a little More
than a little is by much too much" (I:III. ii. 72–73). Implicit everywhere is the unrealized possibility in both man and state of a kind of
Aristotelian norm, an ideal of moderation or of equilibrium among opposing forces.

As these quotations have shown, images from the contemporary psychology of the humors help to shape the larger conceptual framework
of these plays. The centrality of these metaphors is suggested by the
frequency with which characters who fulfill at times a choral role employ
them. It is but a step from fatness to disease. Occasionally rising toward
the end of his life above his absorption in self-pity, Richard prophesies
a growing sickness he failed to cure when he was himself king: the time
will come that "foul sin gathering head Shall break into corruption"
(V. i. 58–59). Meanwhile, as in *Hamlet* (III. iv. 148–149), "rank corruption, mining all within, Infects unseen," and the infection spreads before
it is finally lanced. Henry IV, like Richard before him, becomes increasingly a helpless observer of a malady he cannot cure:

Then you perceive the body of our kingdom,
How foul it is; what rank diseases grow,
And with what danger, near the heart of it. (II:III. i. 38–40)

Henry at least faces more frankly than Richard the fact that he himself
is the sick heart. In Part II, the Archbishop, though a rebel, maintains
a very detached attitude toward the civil war. He speaks of the discontent following the supplanting of Richard by Bolingbroke as a sickness
of the "beastly feeder," the people themselves, who are like dogs that
alternately sate themselves and "disgorge" successive kings: "The commonwealth is sick of their own choice; Their over-greedy love hath sur-
feited" (II. iii. 87–88). Later he includes two reigns and both royalists
and rebels in a general indictment:

we are all diseas'd
And with our surfeiting and wanton hours
Have brought ourselves into a burning fever,
And we must bleed for it; of which disease
Our late King, Richard, being infected, died. (II:IV. i. 54–58)

And, though he disclaims it, he also tries to become England's physician,

> To diet rank minds sick of happiness
> And purge the obstructions which begin to stop
> Our very veins of life.

"Surfeiting" and "wanton" are above all the words for *Richard II*. The disease which begins in the mind of this king spreads to the body of the state and to its noblemen, and the judicious bleeding and purging of England are delayed throughout three plays, until the "mood" (and "mode") is changed, and the "soil" of Henry IV's dubious achievement goes with him into the earth (II:IV. v. 190–200). To trace this creeping infection to its source, a closer analysis of related themes in *Richard II* is now in order.

II

Themes of negligence, excess, and waste are developed in *Richard II* primarily through several strands of imagery—those of time, the garden and sickness, and the farm and death. All are interrelated in a play whose poetic unity has in the last decade been demonstrated many times. When Richard, the state's timekeeper, threatens to appropriate the titles and property which banished Bolingbroke should inherit from John of Gaunt, York sternly equates the rights of inheritance with cosmic law:

> Take Hereford's rights away, and take from Time
> His charters and his customary rights;
> Let not to-morrow then ensue to-day;
> Be not thyself—for how art thou a king
> But by fair sequence and succession?   (II. i. 195–199)

To interrupt the succession of father to son is to endanger the blood descent from king to king, even to unking a rightful sovereign. It is to question the very foundations of what the Gardener (in III. iv) calls "law and form and due proportion," to make time itself have a stop. The suggestion is that "Time" draws up all charters and alone gives them meaning. Within forty lines of this warning we learn that the king is indeed not himself, but "basely led By flatterers . . .," and within a hundred that the discontented nobles have decided to seize the time to "make high majesty look like itself. . . ." Bolingbroke is later accused of having returned to England "Before the expiration of thy time" (the prescribed six years of banishment), and of taking "advantage of the absent time." But Richard's time is "absent" less because he is away in Ireland when Bolingbroke returns than because he has failed to act promptly within it and has abused it. And yet the usurper compounds Richard's crimes. Confronted by the king's loyal friends, Bolingbroke claims "I am a subject, And I challenge law" (II. iii. 133–134). York's reply, however, suggests that Hereford is plucking or seizing (the play's words for the usurper) for his own ends the law and time ignored by Richard. York has had a "feeling" for the injury done Bolingbroke,

> But in this kind to come, in braving arms,
> Be his own carver and cut out his way
> To find out right with wrong—it may not be. . . . (II. iii. 141–145)

Since Richard is himself, as we soon see, a far more clumsy "carver," he is soon cut out of both kingship and kingdom. In the exacting world of the histories, to lose the initiative—or even to act prematurely, like Hotspur—may be to lose one's life. Bolingbroke is above all a master of timing.

Richard dismisses his own folly by invoking divine right. And when he returns from Ireland, the Bishop of Carlisle succinctly phrases the dilemma of the king's taking action:

> Fear not, my lord. That Power that made you king
> Hath power to keep you king in spite of all.
> The means that heaven yields must be embrac'd,
> And not neglected. . . .

If he remains king "in spite of all," Richard surely has no need to rouse himself against the enemy. This doubleness of attitude deeply penetrates the play, for images of inexorability, like those of the rising and falling sun or buckets or of Fortune's wheel, are everywhere contrasted with less fatalistic images of medicine and growth. For nearly two hundred lines at the center of the play, as Richard learns piecemeal that soldiers, subjects, nobles, and favorites have left him, he veers between an exultant characterization of himself as the "Searching eye of heaven" that leaves the guilty "trembling at themselves" (36–62) and a cry of despair: "All souls that will be safe, fly from my side; For time hath set a blot upon my pride" (80–81). He blames the "time," which, like his nobles, the "unruly jades," he could not "manage."

That he himself has abused time Richard finally sees with unusual objectivity in Act V when he is alone in Pomfret:

> How sour sweet music is
> When time is broke and no proportion kept . . . !
> And here have I the daintiness of ear
> To check time broke in a disordered string;
> But, for the concord of my state and time,
> Had not an ear to hear my true time broke.
> I wasted time, and now doth time waste me. . . . (V. v. 42–49)

Few of the kings of the histories have the dainty ear to match royal decree with external event, neither anticipating nor delaying. Dying

Gaunt had hoped that his advice to Richard would "Enforce attention like deep harmony," but York said that Richard's ears were "stopp'd" with flattery. And, opposing deafening "will" to listening "wit," York implied that Richard was out of step with kingdom and self: "all too late comes counsel to be heard Where will doth mutiny with wit's regard" (II. i. 27–28). Richard's inner mutiny renders him unable to maintain the "concord of my state and time," and he falls from wilfulness to will-lessness when first affrighted. Like several other crises in these plays, this fall is enacted simultaneously on the level of plot, character, and language. In the theatre, in the solemn descent from Flint Castle in Act III, stage setting and movement are extensions of verbal imagery. And at Westminister in Act IV Richard's ritualistic speeches and his gestures unkinging himself celebrate, as has been pointed out, a kind of inverse coronation. Incapable of setting firmly the pace of England's affairs, Richard must eventually dance to another's tune. The king who cannot keep time is doomed at the end of the play to become a time-piece: "my time Runs posting on in Bolingbroke's proud joy, While I stand fooling here, his Jack o' th' clock" (V. v. 58–60). And in an elaborately formal figure, the monarch who faced many follies and, finally, outfaced, shatters his mirrored visage at Westminster, reduces himself to a mere clockface, time's "numb'ring clock." Though it has received little attention, the imagery of time is developed and resolved as satisfyingly in Shakespeare's plotting of Richard's decline and fall as the more famous imagery of the sun, which characterizes the sun king's defeat in his pathetic wish: "O that I were a mockery king of snow, Standing before the sun of Bolingbroke . . ." (IV. i. 260–261).

Richard's time is "broke" at the very beginning of the play, and his early folly is also depicted in related images of gardening and sickness. Though the parallels between Richard as gardener and king are developed fully only in the last scene of Act III, they are central to the meaning of the entire drama. The Gardener tells us that Richard, like a careful Adam, should have pruned his garden or state in the spring. The gardeners themselves

> at time of year
> Do wound the bark, the skin of our fruit trees,
> Lest, being over-proud in sap and blood,
> With too much riches it confound itself. (III. iv. 57–60)

The moral of this prudence is pointed up yet more crisply in an allied image from an earlier play. In *2 Henry VI*, Queen Margaret warns Henry of the ambitions of Humphrey of Gloucester:

> Now 'tis the spring, and weeds are shallow-rooted.
> Suffer them now, and they'll o'ergrow the garden
> And choke the herbs for want of husbandry. (III. i. 31–33)

We are reminded of the ancient tithe exacted for God or king at harvest time, as though abundance would breed pride and consequent guilt. Waste and ruin, apparently, are not only the result of human folly but the inevitable outcome of any undisciplined process of nature. Things in a natural state grow too much, and weeds and nobles must be trimmed. But heedless Richard is swarming with caterpillars. One implication of these passages is that a good king must improve on nature by protecting living things (especially himself) against their own excesses. And he must foresee trouble and take his stitch in time. Government demands perpetual wakefulness.

Careless Richard has "suffer'd" a "disordered spring." He has failed to "Cut off the heads of too fast growing sprays That look too lofty in our commonwealth" (III. iv. 34–35). And he has neglected to "root away The noisome weeds" and to trim judiciously: "Superfluous branches We lop away, that bearing boughs may live" (63–64). The thinly disguised political allegory of the garden scene scarcely succeeds in making these remarkable active verbs—"wound," "Cut off," "root away," and "lop away" (when applied to "great and growing men")—very palatable to the modern reader. But Shakespeare takes his often daring analogues between the king, the state, and external nature as seriously here as in the major tragedies, which imply a very different ethic. The Gardener, whose formal speech suggests that he has a choral function as a kind of alter-ego for Richard, states that Richard should have acted "like an executioner," for now "our sea-walled garden, the whole land, Is full of weeds, her fairest flowers chok'd up . . ." (43–44). But at the very beginning of the play, the sternness of this duty of the king is contrasted sharply with Richard's indecisiveness. Richard there attempts to resolve the "swelling difference" between Bolingbroke and Mowbray, not by the "Justice" of a traditional duel, but by banishment. At first, as the blank verse of the first scene shifts suddenly into rhyme, he chants

> Let's purge this choler without letting blood.
> This we prescribe, though no physician;
> Deep malice makes too deep incision.
> Forget, forgive; conclude and be agreed;
> Our doctors say this is no month to bleed. (153–157)

Like a physician maintaining a balance among the body's humors, however, Richard should promptly have made a "deep incision" to "purge" blood overproud and too rich, just as the precautionary Gardener wounds the bark of his fruit trees. The parallel is explicit: tapping is bleeding, and both as gardener and as doctor Richard is negligent. Even Gaunt's solicitations for his son fail to account fully for Richard's stopping of the duel at Coventry in the third scene, "for," as Richard says, "our eyes do hate the dire aspect Of civil wounds plough'd up with neighbors' sword . . ." (127–128). This is the moment to "check time broke" and the "too fast growing sprays," but Richard is not listening.

That Richard's eyes have not always hated civil wounds is made clear in the somber colloquy which takes place between these first and third scenes of chivalric challenging. Here the Duchess of Gloucester tells us of Richard's hand in the death of his uncle Woodstock, who was "crack'd, and all the precious liquor spilt . . . By envy's hand and murder's bloody axe" (19, 21). And old Gaunt, recalling this political murder later, asks Richard not to spare the blood which they all derive from Edward III: "That blood already, like the pelican, Hast thou tapp'd out and drunkenly carous'd" (II. i. 126–127). Richard has failed to bleed when he should and has tapped and drunk the family blood he should have preserved. Had he bled the "great and growing men" in time, the Gardener tells us, "They might have liv'd to bear, and he to taste Their fruits of duty" (III. iv. 62–63). But there is neither healthy bearing nor fruit in Richard's garden; his land has no "hope to grow" (III. ii. 212). And his successor, who greatly exceeds Richard's crimes by plucking out a king "planted many years" and by "grafting" new plants, reaps a "field of Golgotha and dead men's skulls" (IV. i. 144).

In still other closely related groups of images, Richard's garden becomes a farm and his land his deathbed. In Gaunt's most famous speech and in several passages on divine right, the play gives us two of the most exalted pictures of England and the divinity of kingship in Shakespeare. But by Act II both have fallen from high estate. Gaunt proceeds from his praise of "This other Eden, demi-paradise," to a terrible indictment. "This blessed plot" is "now leas'd out . . . Like to a tenement or pelting farm" (II. i. 59–60).[2] It is bound in not with the "triumphant sea," which keeps it from "infection," but with "inky blots and rotten parchment bonds," and thus the conqueror of others "Hath made a shameful conquest of itself" (64, 66). The "customary rights" of time have become opportunistic "parchment bonds," and Richard robs his land as he robs his cousin. Gaunt is eloquent about the crime of turning a royal realm into real estate: "Why, cousin, wert thou regent of the world, It were a shame to let this land by lease . . ." (109–110). As the demi-paradise becomes a farm, the king becomes a mere overlord: "Landlord of England art thou now, not King. Thy state of law is bond-slave to the law . . ." (113–114). This businessman is a far cry from the "deputy elected by the Lord," whom Richard later says the "breath of worldly men cannot depose . . ." (III. ii. 56–57). When the shrill chorus

---

2 In his suggestive edition of *Woodstock* (London, 1946), A. P. Rossiter points out that Shakespeare not only carries over word for word many of these charges from the earlier play, but takes "as read" in *Woodstock* a complicity with Mowbray in Gloucester's death which weakens Richard's judgment of the contest in Act I. See pp. 47–53, 198, 225–226. [See also the essay on *Richard II* in the same author's *Angel with Horns* (London, 1961).]

of nobles denounces Richard's commercial exploitation of a sacred trust, we are reminded of the threat to the state in *1 Henry IV* when the rebels propose to divide England or of Lear's "darker purpose" in dividing his kingdom. "The King's grown bankrout, like a broken man," the nobles cry, and "Reproach and dissolution hangeth over him" (II. i. 257–258). In ravaging his realm Richard is ravaging his subjects: "The commons hath he pill'd with grievous taxes And quite lost their hearts . . ." (246–247). And the old word "pill'd" (stripped bare, peeled) leads us to the central group of metaphors in which Richard is seen as destroying himself.

The Gardener speaks of the "wholesome herbs Swarming with caterpillars," and in one of the speeches in the play which unite several of its major strands of imagery, Gaunt identifies the sickness of the king with that of his land. In metaphors like these, perhaps for the first time, Shakespeare has brought the chronicle of a king and of his kingdom into perfect unity.

> Thy deathbed is no lesser than thy land,
> Wherein thou liest in reputation sick. . . . (II. i. 95–96)

The doctor who should be bleeding the sick body of the realm is himself laid out sick upon it, at the mercy of the physicians who "first wounded" him.

> A thousand flatterers sit within thy crown,
> Whose compass is no bigger than thy head;
> And yet, incaged in so small a verge,
> The waste is no whit lesser than thy land. (100–103)

The waste (waist) of the king's "Controlling majesty" is the waste of the state. The caterpillars (an Elizabethan commonplace for flattering parasites like Bushy and company), by eating away Richard's power to govern, are devouring the green garden of England. In a similar metaphor, Richard himself later sees his crown as his court, destroyed by idle courtiers. The decline of crown, court, and land is simultaneous. But, unwilling to admit that his principal enemy is his own indulgence, represented by his minions, Richard extravagantly views his real opponent as death, who is merely marking time until he strikes. This illusion is developed in several remarkable figures.

Even before he meets Bolingbroke at Flint Castle, Richard—projecting his own faults, perhaps, and posing them as an implacable abstract enemy—gives us his own version of Gaunt's deathbed warning: "within the hollow crown That rounds the mortal temples of a king Keeps Death his court . . ." (III. ii. 160–162). The folly Richard has not governed is personified and seen as governing him. Death allows the king to "mon-archize" and infuses him with conceit, as if flesh were

> brass impregnable; and humour'd thus,
> Comes at the last, and with a little pin
> Bores through his castle wall, and farewell king! (168–170)

These images parallel the Gardener's, of Richard as a tree in England's garden, surrounded by "weeds which his broad-spreading leaves did shelter, That seem'd in eating him to hold him up . . ." (III. ii. 50–51). The "sea-walled garden" of Gaunt's speech and the Gardener's, the "flinty ribs" of Flint and Pomfret, and even the divinity that hedges kings cannot defend against himself the guilty monarch who "With nothing shall be pleas'd till he be eas'd With being nothing" (V. v. 40–41). Self-pitying Richard rarely associates his own suffering of the weeds with the doom he views as inexorable. In this respect and others he lacks the stature of the later tragic heroes. Rationalizing the effects of his negli-gence as necessity, Richard perhaps sees himself, the physician, dieted and bled by death. He implies that he could confront the sword of Bolingbroke, but is clearly helpless before the "little pin." "Subjected thus," Richard cries, "How can you say to me I am a king" (III. ii. 176–177)? On his way to the Tower after he is deposed, he tells the queen, "I am sworn brother, sweet, To grim Necessity, and he and I Will keep a league till death" (V. i. 20–22). This is divine right turned strangely upside down: can't be deposed becomes must be. But there are several indications in the play that Richard cannot really believe in this right, in himself, or in his kingdom.

Bolingbroke crisply observes after Richard has lost power that the shadow of Richard's sorrow has destroyed the shadow of his face. He thereby emphasizes the unreal character of both the kingly fears and the fair "show" of the man who "looks" like a king (III. iii. 67–71). Richard's world as king is as fanciful as the thoughts which people his "little world" when he is alone in Pomfret. The weeds and caterpillars which begin to "eat" him are like the generations of "still-breeding thoughts" (IV. v. 8) in his head, for both breed only destruction. In one sense, Richard himself is probably Death, tapping out with a little pin the life he cannot govern. The actual threats to the state seem half-shaped by the sick fears of the king, and its later crises partly mirror his fall within his own mind from false security to helpless self-division. This play, dominated by the imagery of excess, presents in its central character a man who turns from an extreme of posturing bravado to passive weeping and finds no kingly norm between. He leaves the seat of a kingdom to "sit upon the ground And tell sad stories of the death of kings" (III. ii. 155–156). He abandons a land "Dear for her reputation through the world" for a "little little grave, an obscure grave," and he becomes his own "tomb." In the language of the play, Richard "melts" away, and we recall Gaunt's stern warning: "Light vanity, insatiate cormorant, Consuming means, soon preys upon itself" (II. i. 38–39).

III

Richard's failure as watchful gardener and physician bequeaths to his successor a realm fat and very sick. The grieving queen suggests an intimate cause-and-effect relationship between the two reigns when she fancies herself giving birth to Bolingbroke, her "sorrow's dismal heir" (II. ii. 62), almost as though he were begotten by Richard's folly. But the play's poetic justice is not so simple. Bolingbroke's watchful shrewdness collaborates with Richard's ineffectuality to turn Fortune's wheel. The two men, like other protagonists in Shakespeare, are functions of each other and of their total situation. They are locked in a grim dance in which Richard's weakness opens the way to power for Bolingbroke, and Bolingbroke's silent strength matches Richard's expectations of annihilation. Metaphors of water and of moving buckets suggest a Bolingbroke on high poised and ready to flood a royal reservoir that empties itself. But judgments in the later histories are kinder to the wastrel Richard than to the politician Bolingbroke, whose usurpation and killing of a king are thought more heinous than all of Richard's folly. Though a trimmer, Bolingbroke cannot weed his own garden, for his foes are "enrooted with his friends . . ." (II:IV. i. 207). In a long speech to Prince Hal in 1 Henry IV, troubled Henry sees Richard's blind rioting recapitulated in his son, perhaps as a punishment for Henry's own "misreadings." This comparison between Richard and Hal affords us a convenient vantage point for pursuing thematic imagery of waste and excess through succeeding plays of this group. Analysis will be centered upon three or four critical passages and the character of Falstaff.

After the excesses of Richard's reign, the Lancastrians reject fatness and imprudence in both man and commonwealth. This rejection underlies the famous first interview of Henry with his son, the Prince's first soliloquy, and the Prince's later banishment of Falstaff. Henry tells Hal that when he himself courted the crown, his own state, "Seldom but sumptuous, show'd like a feast And won by rareness such solemnity" (III. ii. 57–59). The politician's view of public appearance as strategy could scarcely be further refined. In sixty-odd lines, Henry employs "seldom" three times to refer to his activities and reenforces it with a dozen other words suggesting economy. In a score of very different terms, however, Henry says that men were with King Richard's presence "glutted, gorg'd, and full," for he,

> being daily swallowed by men's eyes,
> They surfeited with honey and began
> To loathe the taste of sweetness. . . . (70–72, 84)

Kingship is here a kind of candy which should be given the people in-
frequently, probably when one wishes something from them. Three of
Henry's verbs are especially significant:

> And then I stole all courtesy from heaven,
> And dress'd myself in such humility
> That I did pluck allegiance from men's hearts. . . . (50–52)

It is unnecessary to apply these words to Hal to observe that his seldom-
ness (and his careful "dress") has something in common with that of his
father. Indeed, as prince (though not as king), his seldom-acting in the
interests of the state is rather like Henry's seldom-appearing, but it
commits him to greater personal risks.

Though Hal spends his youth as a madcap of "unyok'd humour" de-
siring small beer and as a friend of the "trunk of humours," he seems
to know from the beginning what he is doing. In his first soliloquy (I. ii.
219–241) he exhibits the theatrical sense of timing of other Shakespearian heroes, sharpened to a remarkable degree. He says he will
"imitate the sun" which "doth permit" the clouds to "smother up his
beauty," so that his eventual shining will be "more wonder'd at." One
of his figures about holidays employs his father's terms: "when they
seldom come, they wish'd-for come, And nothing pleaseth but rare accidents." He wants his reformation to "show more goodly and attract
more eyes Than that which hath no foil to set it off." This is surely the
returning prodigal calculating every effect: he will "offend to make
offence a skill." Part of this attitude derives from the emphasis upon
absoluteness in the heroic code, according to which it is no "sin to covet
honor," and "Two stars" cannot "share" in glory (I:V. iv. 64–65). It derives also from the necessity of the protagonist in Shakespeare to have a
"dainty" ear, from his necessity to collaborate in the nick of time with
his fate: "the readiness is all." "Percy is but my factor . . .," the Prince
tells his father,

> To engross up glorious deeds on my behalf;
> And I will call him to so strict account
> That he shall render every glory up. . . . (I:III. ii. 147–150)

Bolingbroke's earlier imagery of "more" and "less" here becomes finan-
cial. This young accountant will appear to be eating and sleeping, but
when Hotspur's bond of honor has matured, Hal will spring to life and
exact both principal and interest, "Or I will tear the reckoning from his
heart" (152). Behind this ferocity of course lies the ancient notion of
the conqueror's (like the cannibal's) gaining the strength and virtue of
the conquered. But the Prince's accounting reminds us of the very
different "trim reckoning" by which Falstaff reduces honor to a word,
and we must turn to the knight who only reckons his sack to understand

more fully why the Prince seems to be eating his cake and having it too.

When Henry V banishes the "tutor and the feeder of my riots" at the end of Part II, he speaks of his companionship with Falstaff as a "dream," which—"being awak'd" and watching for sleeping England—he now despises (II:V. v. 53–55). The younger Henry apparently dreams of Falstaff as Richard II seemed to dream of Bolingbroke in England's garden, but unlike Richard, he does not succumb to his nightmare. Some critics have been offended by an image (among others) from Henry's rejection speech which the metaphors we have been following should help to deepen and justify: "Make less thy body, hence, and more thy grace; Leave gormandizing" (56–57). To throw these words and this controversial scene into larger perspective, we must give appropriate emphasis to the virtues of law and order embodied in the Chief Justice and of prudence and economy running through all of the histories. And we must remember the surprising seriousness with which Falstaff defends himself and the Prince promises to banish him ("I do, I will") during the mock interview—really the trial of a way of life—in Part I (II. iv. 462–528). Both seem to know from the beginning that this dream will end. But the complexity of Falstaff and of our attitudes toward him is the best measure of the delicate balance among political and moral attitudes maintained throughout these plays.

The sympathy of the world has always been with the fat knight, and the popularity of these plays would be vastly reduced if, unimaginably, he were not in them. The Prince's turning from "plump Jack," "All the world," can be seen as the rejection of fuller life in favor of power, of being for becoming. That Jack is perhaps an inevitable companion for the Prince, Henry IV makes plain when he associates fatness with nobility in speaking of his son: "Most subject is the fattest soil to weeds; And he, the noble image of my youth, Is overspread with them" (II:IV. iv. 54–56). But in a comic but highly significant defense of the medicine he recommends for every illness, Falstaff says that the royal blood or soil in Hal was originally "lean, sterile, and bare" and had to be "manured, husbanded, and till'd" with "fertile sherris" to make Hal "valiant" (II:IV. iii. 92–135). Falstaff's phenomenal attractiveness and his mockery of honor and all state affairs give us, among other things, just the insight we need into the "cold blood" of the Lancasters, and also into the dying chivalric code for which his "catechism" (I:V. i. 128–140) is a kind of epitaph or *reductio ad absurdum*. But the parallels between the sustained imagery we have been following and Shakespeare's characterization of Falstaff emphasize a darker side of this hill of flesh and illuminate his profoundly functional role in this entire cycle of plays.

Far from threatening the structure of the histories, as some have maintained, Falstaff is one of their central organizing symbols. It is tempting to guess that Shakespeare rapidly found the imagery drawn from nature and animal life which is so marked a feature of the style of *Henry VI* and, far more subtly and intricately, of *Richard II,* inadequate for his increasingly complicated meanings. However we account for it, he developed or chanced upon another and far more expressive vehicle for the ideas of the sick state and king associated in *Richard II* with the overgrown garden. The final evolution of the metaphor of the fat garden and of the sick body politic is probably the fat man. Metaphors from the unweeded garden may underline or even symbolize the sickness of the realm, to be sure, but the tun of man can also, if as alert and witty as Falstaff, make the best possible case for fatness, for the "sin" of being "old and merry," for "instinct" and life rather than grinning honor and death. And he can afford us the point of view from which thinness and economy can be seen as inadequate or unpleasant characteristics. Thus he can throw into clearer relief the entire political and personal ethic of the histories. If we compare the relatively simple equivalence between the physical ugliness of the "elvish-mark'd, abortive, rooting hog," Richard III, and the disordered state, on the one hand, with the ambivalent richness of the relationships between the "shapes" of Falstaff and rebellious England, on the other, we can have a helpful index of the deepening of Shakespeare's thought and his growing mastery of his medium over the five or six years (1592–3 to 1597–8) that separate the first of the major histories from the greatest.

Falstaff, then, is both the sickness of the state, the prince of the caterpillars preying on the commonwealth, and the remedy for some of its ills. And his role dramatizes the gulf between the essential virtues of the private man and those of the ruler, for as we see in *Antony,* the feast which nourishes the one often sickens the other. Timeless Falstaff is in a curiously reciprocal relationship with time-serving Henry IV, for they are the principal competitors for the Prince's allegiance, in affording by precept and example radically contrasting mirrors for the young magistrate. But the usurper who disdained to follow the example of rioting Richard, as we have seen, finds his eldest son rioting with Falstaff —a kind of embodiment of Henry's inability to weed his own garden. Both the politician and the reveler must disappear from the world of young Henry V before he can find his own voice somewhere between them. He had to befriend Falstaff to know this man's gifts and "language," and in the "perfectness of time" he had to act to arrest the threat of such "gross terms" to the kingdom (II:IV. iv. 68–75). The threat is real, for Falstaff is almost the result of a process similar to that referred to by the Archbishop in defending the rebels in Part II: "The time misord'red doth, in common sense, Crowd us and crush us to this monstrous form . . ." (II:IV. ii. 33–34). We can hardly sentimentalize a Falstaff who says he will "turn diseases to commodity" (II:I. ii. 277), when we remember the Bastard's great attack upon "commodity" (op-

portunism, time-serving) in the nearly contemporary *King John*.[3] And
we cannot ignore the outrageousness of Falstaff's cry upon hearing of
Hal's succession, just before he himself is banished: "Let us take any
man's horses; the laws of England are at my commandment" (II:V. iii.
141–142). Falstaff threatens to usurp the "customary rights" of time,
governed as he says he is only by the moon, and to make the law
"bondslave" to lawlessness.

Falstaff is depicted in language very similar to that employed in two
of the most vivid pictures of disorder in all of Shakespeare, both of them
from *2 Henry IV*. Once in a kind of mock despair, the wily Northumberland prays that "order die! And let this world no longer be a stage
To feed contention in a ling'ring act . . ." (I. i. 154–156). Later, the
dying king, apprehensive lest his realm receive the "scum" of "neighbour
confines" and become a "wilderness," fears that Hall will

> Pluck down my officers, break my decrees;
> For now a time is come to mock at form.
> Harry the Fifth is crown'd. Up, vanity . . . !
> For the Fifth Harry from curb'd license plucks
> The muzzle of restraint, and the wild dog
> Shall flesh his tooth on every innocent. (IV. v. 118–20, 131–133)

The formless man, "vanity in years," who has mocked at all forms of
honor has been the prince's closest companion, potentially a powerful
voice in state affairs. The real target of the "fool and jester" has been
the "rusty curb of old father antic the law" (I:I. ii. 69–70), and the violence in the lines above of "wild dog" and "flesh" reminds us of the
"butcher" of the histories, Richard III, and of the cormorant-villains of
the tragedies. The rejection of Falstaff marks the new king's turning
from the negligence and excess that had nearly destroyed England since
the reign of Richard II. As the young king dismisses one tutor and
embraces another in the Chief Justice, he cultivates his garden in "law
and form and due proportion":

> The tide of blood in me
> Hath proudly flow'd in vanity till now.
> Now doth it turn and ebb back to the sea,
> Where it shall mingle with the state of floods
> And flow henceforth in formal majesty. (II:V. ii. 129–133)

The proud river of the private will has become the sea of life of the
commonwealth. The blood which here as in the tragedies is the basis of
both mood and mind is purged. The man who said he was of all humors

[3] As has frequently been observed, the Falstaff of Part II is a less complicated and attractive
figure than the Falstaff of Part I. Increasingly obsessed with his age, his aches and diseases,
and, being rarely in the company of the Prince, at once more arrogant and less witty, he
seems to embody less of the high-spiritedness which the Lancastrians lack and more of the
corruption which threatens to engulf the kingdom.

comes to achieve the "finely bolted" balance which Henry once thought characterized the traitor Scroop:

> spare in diet,
> Free from gross passion or of mirth or anger . . .
> Not working with the eye without the ear,
> And but in purged judgment trusting neither. (*H.V.*, II. ii. 131–136)

Henry V is by no means the kind of hero we would admire fully in the tragedies. But the Choruses which celebrate his virtues make perfectly plain that this trim watcher rises from his father's vain engrossing of "cank'red heaps" of gold to genuine magnanimity—the fearless sun king:

> A largess universal, like the sun,
> His liberal eye doth give to every one,
> Thawing cold fear. (Pro. 4. 43–45)

HAROLD JENKINS

The Structural Problem in Shakespeare's Henry the Fourth

. . . The first problem that confronts one in approaching *Henry IV,* and the one about which I propose to be particular, has inevitably introduced itself already. Is it one play or two? Some of you will dismiss this as an academic question, the sort of thing that only people like professors bother their heads about. Some of you will look askance at it as a metaphysical question, which in a sense it is. But it is also, surely, a practical question: how satisfactorily can either the first part or the second be shown in the theatre without the other? What is gained, or indeed lost, by presenting the two parts, as the Old Vic are doing at the moment, on successive evenings? And thus of course the question becomes a problem of literary criticism. Until it has been answered, how can the dramatic quality of *Henry IV* be fully appreciated, or even defined? Yet the numerous literary critics who have attempted an answer to the question have reached surprisingly opposite conclusions.

Answers began more than two hundred years ago in the *Critical Observations on Shakespeare* by John Upton, a man who deserves our regard for trying to scotch the notion so strangely current in the eighteenth century that "Shakespeare had no learning." Far from accepting that Shakespeare's plays were the happy, or the not so happy, products of untutored nature, Upton maintained that they were constructed according to some principles of art; and his examination of *Henry IV* suggested to him that each of its two parts had, what Aristotle of course demanded, its own beginning, middle, and end. Upton held it to be an injury to Shakespeare even to speak of a first and second *part* and thus conceal the fact that there were here two quite independent plays.[1] To this Dr Johnson retorted that these two plays, so far from being inde-

From a lecture delivered at Westfield College, University of London (1955); printed as a bound volume by Methuen & Company (1956). Reprinted by permission of Methuen & Company Ltd. and of the author. The version reprinted here is slightly abridged.

[1] *Op. cit.*, 1746. See especially pp. 11, 41–2, 70–1.

pendent, are "two only because they are too long to be one." They could
appear as separate plays, he thought, only to those who looked at them
with the "ambition of critical discoveries." In these tart words Johnson
shrewdly defined what if not one of the deadly sins, is still a vice and
one to which universities are prone. The "ambition of critical discoveries," a natural human vanity unnaturally nourished in our day by the
requirements of the Ph.D. thesis and the demand for "publications,"
has been responsible for many interpretations of Shakespeare whose
merit is in their being new rather than their being true. Yet one must
not always accept the accepted. Dr Johnson's contemporaries did
not all find it as plain as he did that *Henry IV* was just one continuous
composition. It seemed probable to Malone that Part 2 was not even
"conceived"[2] until Part 1 had been a roaring success. Capel, on the
other hand, thought that both parts were "planned at the same time,
and with great judgment."[3]

Among present-day scholars Professor Dover Wilson is on Johnson's
side. He insists that the two parts of *Henry IV* are "a single structure"
with the "normal dramatic curve" stretched over ten acts instead of five.
Professor R. A. Law, however, declares that *Henry IV* is "not a single
ten-act play," but two organic units "written with different purposes in
view." On the contrary, says Dr Tillyard, "The two parts of the play
are a single organism." Part 1 by itself is "patently incomplete." "Each
part is a drama complete in itself," says Kittredge flatly.[4] In short, some
two centuries after Upton and Johnson, scholars are still about equally
divided as to whether *Henry IV* was "planned" as "one long drama" or
whether the second part was, as they put it, an "unpremeditated sequel."
A new professor, his ambition already dwindling at Johnson's warning,
might well lapse into melancholy, or even modesty. Modest or not, he
can hardly escape the conclusion, reached by another eighteenth-century
dignitary in a somewhat different situation, that "much might be said
on both sides." Like Sir Roger de Coverley, he "would not give his
judgment rashly," yet like the late R. W. Chambers, whose pupil I am
proud to have been, he may think that the modesty which forbears to
make a judgment is disastrous.[5]

Words like "planned" and "unpremeditated" figure largely in this controversy; and of course they imply intention or the lack of it, and will
therefore be suspect in those circles which denounce what is called "the
intentional fallacy."[6] I am far from belonging to that school of criticism
which holds that an author's own intention is irrelevant to our reading

2 *Shakespeare,* Johnson-Steevens Variorum, 2nd edn., 1778, i. 300.
3 *Notes and Various Readings to Shakespeare,* [1775], p. 164.
4 *1 Henry IV,* ed. Kittredge, 1940, p. viii.
5 See *Beowulf, an Introduction to the Study of the Poem,* 2nd edn., 1932, p. 390.
6 This is actually the title of an article by W. K. Wimsatt and M. C. Beardsley in the
Sewanee Review, LIV (1946), 468 ff., repr. in Wimsatt's *The Verbal Icon,* 1954.

of his work; yet, as Lascelles Abercrombie says, aesthetic criticism must ultimately judge by results: a man's work is evidence of what he did, but you can never be sure what he intended.[7] This position, with the coming of the Freudian psychology, is finally inescapable, but in its extreme form it seems to me unnecessarily defeatist. When I find *Much Ado About Nothing* beginning with talk of a battle in which those killed are "few of any sort, and none of name," I may infer that Shakespeare intended to write a comedy and not a realistic one at that. But if I wish to play for safety, I may use a phrase of Lascelles Abercrombie's own and speak—not of what Shakespeare intended, but of what he "warned his audience to expect."[8] If we leave aside for the present all question of Shakespeare's intention, what does *Henry IV* itself, as it begins and proceeds along its course, warn us to expect?

The short first scene, filled with reports of wars—wars this time in which multitudes are "butchered"—makes an apt beginning for a history play. But its dialogue announces no main action. Yet certain topics, brought in with apparent casualness, naturally engage our interest. There is talk of two young men who do not yet appear, both called "young Harry," yet apparently unlike. The first of them, Hotspur, is introduced as "gallant," an epithet which is very soon repeated when he is said to have won "a gallant prize." The prisoners he has taken are, we are told, "a conquest for a prince to boast of." Already, before Prince Hal is even named, a contrast is being begun between a man who behaves like a prince though he is not one and another who is in fact a prince but does not act the part. The King makes this explicit. Hotspur, who has gained "an honourable spoil," is "a son who is the theme of honour's tongue," while the King's own son is stained with "riot and dishonour." In the second and third scenes the two Harries in turn appear. First, the Prince, already associated with dishonour, instead of, like Hotspur, taking prisoners in battle, plans to engage in highway robbery. Then, when he has arranged to sup next night in a tavern, he is followed on the stage by Hotspur telling how, when he took his prisoners, he was "dry with rage and extreme toil." This practice of juxtaposing characters who exhibit opposite codes of conduct is a common one in Shakespeare's drama. After the "unsavoury similes" that Hal swaps with Falstaff, in which a squalling cat and a stinking ditch are prominent, there is Hotspur's hyperbole about plucking "bright honour from the pale-faced moon." It may not be a classical construction, but there is enough suggestion here of arrangement to justify Upton's claim for Shakespeare's art. We expect that central to the play will be the antithesis between these two young men and the lives they lead. And we shall find that this antithesis precipitates a moral contest

---

[7] *A Plea for the Liberty of Interpreting*, British Acad. Shakespeare Lecture, 1930, p. 6.
[8] *Ibid.*, p. 22.

which is an important aspect of the historical action of the drama.

The historical action presents Hotspur's rebellion. It is an action which develops with a fine structural proportion throughout Part 1. The act divisions, although they are not Shakespeare's of course, being first found in the Folio, may serve nevertheless as a convenient register of the way the action is disposed. In the first act the rebel plot is hatched, in the second Hotspur prepares to leave home, in the third he joins forces with the other rebel leaders, in the fourth the rebel army is en-camped ready to give battle, in the fifth it is defeated and Hotspur is killed. Meantime, along with the military contest between Hotspur and the King, the moral contest between the Prince and Hotspur proceeds with an equally perfect balance. The opposition of honour and riot established in the first act is intensified in the second, where a scene of Hotspur at home preparing for war is set against one of Hal revelling in the tavern. The revelry even includes a little skit by Hal on Hotspur's conversation with his wife, which serves not only to adjust our view of Hotspur's honour by subjecting it to ridicule, but also to emphasize that the Prince is—with gleeful understatement—"not yet of Percy's mind." That he is not of Percy's mind leads the King in the third act to resume his opening plaint: it is not the Prince but Percy, with his "never-dying honour," who is fit to be a king's son. At this point the Prince vows to outshine his rival. He will meet "this gallant Hotspur"—the words echo the opening scene—this "child of honour," and overcome him. And so, when the rebels see the Prince in Act 4, he is "gallantly arm'd"—Hot-spur's word is now applied to him—and he vaults upon his horse "as if an angel dropp'd down from the clouds"—with a glory, that is, already beyond Hotspur. All that then remains is that the Prince shall demon-strate his new chivalry in action, which of course he does in the fifth act, first saving his father's life and finally slaying Hotspur in single combat. Opposed to one another throughout the play, constantly spoken of together, these two are nevertheless kept apart till the fifth act, when their first and last encounter completes in the expected manner the pattern of their rivalry that began in the opening words. The two have exchanged places. Supremacy in honour has passed from Hotspur to the Prince, and the wayward hero of the opening ends by exhibiting his true princely nature.

What then is one to make of the view of Professor Dover Wilson that the Battle of Shrewsbury, in which the Prince kills Hotspur, is not an adequate conclusion but merely the "nodal point we expect in a third act"? If we do expect a "nodal point" in a third act, then *Henry IV* Part 1 will not disappoint us. For there *is* a nodal point, and—I am tempted to say this categorically—it is in the third act of Part 1 that it occurs. In this third act, when the King rebukes his son, the Prince replies, "I will redeem all this . . ."; in the fifth act he fulfils this vow at Shrewsbury, as is signalized by the King's admission that the Prince has "redeem'd" his "lost opinion." Again, in the third act, the Prince swears that he will take from Hotspur "every honour sitting on his helm"; in the fifth act Hotspur is brought to confess that the Prince has won "proud titles" from him.[9] More significantly still, the third act ends

with the Prince saying,

> *Percy stands on high;*
> *And either we or they must lower lie;*

and then the fifth act shows us the spectacle of the hero looking down upon his rival's prostrate form. The curve of the plot could hardly be more firmly or more symmetrically drawn. It does not seem easy to agree with Dr Johnson and Professor Dover Wilson that *Henry IV* Part 1 is only the first half of a play.

If this were all there were to *Henry IV* Part 1, the matter would be simple. But the Prince's conquest of honour is only one aspect of his progress; the other is his break with the companions of his riots. Interwoven with the story of the Prince and Hotspur are the Prince's relations with Falstaff, and these, from Falstaff's first appearance in the second scene of the play, are presented in a way which leads us to expect a similar reversal. The essential thing about Hal is that, scapegrace that he is, he is the future king—the "true prince," the "sweet young prince," the "king's son," the "heir apparent," as Falstaff variously calls him, with whatever degree of mockery, in their first dialogue together. More than that, this dialogue is constantly pointing forward to the moment when he will come to the throne. "When thou art king,"— Falstaff uses these words four times in the first seventy lines and yet again before the scene is over. "Shall there be gallows standing in England when thou art king?" "Do not thou, when thou art king, hang a thief." And so on. With these words ringing in our ears, then, we are continually being reminded of what is to come. The words seem, however, to refer to some vague time in the distant future. The Prince's reign will inescapably become reality, but it is at present apprehended as a dream. Falstaff's irrepressible fancy blows up a vast gaily-coloured bubble, and as Bradley recognized,[10] it is because this bubble encloses the dreams of all of us that we feel for Falstaff so much affection. In our dreams we all do exactly as we like, and the date of their realization is to be when Hal is king. Then, everything will be changed—except of course ourselves. *We* shall go on as before, our friend Falstaff will continue his nocturnal depredations, but highwaymen will not be regarded as thieves and punishments will be abolished. Unfortunately, in the real

9 The connection here is reinforced by the Prince's use of his earlier image: "all the budding honours on thy crest I'll crop."
10 "The Rejection of Falstaff," *Oxford Lectures on Poetry*, 1909, pp. 262–3.

world outside the bubble, it is not the law but we ourselves that should change, as Falstaff recognizes when he says, "I must give over this life, and I will give it over. . . I'll be damned for never a king's son in Christendom." The joke of this is that we know that Falstaff will never give over, nor means to; but the joke does not quite conceal the seriousness of the alternatives—give over or be damned; and the idea of damnation continues to dance before us, now and later, in further jests about Falstaff's selling his soul to the devil, wishing to repent, and having to "give the devil his due." What Falstaff's eventual doom is to be could be discerned more than dimly by a mind that came to this play unfurnished by literature or folk-lore. And none of us is quite as innocent as that. We cannot help being aware of an archetypal situation in which a man dallies with a diabolical tempter whom he either renounces or is destroyed by; and to the first audience of *Henry IV* this situation was already familiar in a long line of Christian plays, in some of which man's succumbing to temptation was symbolized in his selling his soul to the devil and being carried off to Hell. It is because it is so familiar that it is readily accepted as matter for jesting, while the jests give a hint of Falstaff's role in the play. I merely pick out one or two threads in the very complex fabric of the dialogue: you will be good enough, I trust, to believe that, in spite of some dubious precedents in the recent criticism of other plays, I am not seeking to interpret *Henry IV* as an allegory of sin and damnation. Falstaff is not a type-figure, though within his vast person several types are contained. And one of them is a sinner and provokes many piquant allusions to the typical fate of sinners, whether on the earthly gallows or in the infernal fire. There is also an ambiguity, to use the modern jargon, which permits Falstaff to be not only the sinner but the tempter as well. The jokes of a later scene will call him indeed a devil who haunts the Prince, a "reverend vice," an "old white-bearded Satan." What I think the play makes clear from the beginning is that neither as sinner nor as tempter will Falstaff come to triumph. Even as we share his dream of what will happen when Hal is king, we confidently await the bursting of his bubble.

To strengthen our expectation even further is what we know of history, or at least of that traditional world where the territories of history and legend have no clear boundaries. The peculiarity of the history play is that while pursuing its dramatic ends, it must also obey history and steer a course reasonably close to an already known pattern of events. The story of Prince Hal was perfectly familiar to the Elizabethan audience before the play began, and it was the story of a prince who had a madcap youth, including at least one escapade of highway robbery, and then, on succeeding to the throne, banished his riotous companions from court and became the most valorous king England had ever had. Not only was this story vouched for in the chronicles, but it had already found its way on to the stage, as an extant play, *The Famous Victories of Henry the Fifth,* bears witness, in however garbled a text. It is hardly open to *our* play, then, to depart from the accepted pattern, in which the banishment of the tavern friends is an essential feature. Moreover, that they are to be banished the Prince himself assures us at the end of his first scene with Poins and Falstaff in that soliloquy which generations of critics have made notorious.

> I know you all, and will awhile uphold
> The unyoked humour of your idleness.

The word "awhile" plants its threat of a different time to come when a "humour" now "unyoked" will be brought under restraint. The soliloquy tells us as plain as any prologue what the end of the play is to be.

Yet although *Henry IV* Part 1 thus from its first act directs our interest to the time when Hal will be king, it is not of course until the last act of Part 2 that Pistol comes to announce, "Sir John, thy tender lambkin now is king." It is not until the last act of Part 2 that the Prince is able to institute the new régime which makes mock of Falstaff's dreamworld. And it is not of course till the final scene of all that the newly crowned king makes his ceremonial entrance and pronounces the words that have threatened since he and Falstaff first were shown together. "I banish thee." To all that has been said about the rejection of Falstaff I propose to add very little. The chief of those who objected to it, Bradley himself, recognized the necessity of it while complaining of how it was done. Granted that the new king had to drop his former friend, might he not have spared him the sermon and parted from him in private?[11] Yet Professor Dover Wilson is surely right to maintain that the public utterance is the essential thing.[12] From the first, as I have shown, interest is concentrated on the prince as the future sovereign and Falstaff builds hopes on the nature of his rule. Their separation, when it comes, is not then a reluctant parting between friends, but a royal decree promulgated with due solemnity. This is also the perfect moment for it, when the crown that has hovered over the hero from the beginning is seen, a striking symbol in the theatre, fixed firmly on his head. The first words of the rejection speech elevate him still further—"I know thee not" —for the scriptural overtones here[13] make the speaker more than a king. The situation presents many aspects, but one of them shows the tempter vanquished and another the sinner cast into outer darkness. In either case the devil, we may say, gets his due.

The last act of Part 2 thus works out a design which is begun in the first act of Part 1. How then can we agree with Kittredge that each part

11 *Ibid.,* p. 253.
12 *The Fortunes of Falstaff,* pp. 120–1.
13 *Cf.* Luke xiii. 25–7.

is a complete play? Such a pronouncement fits the text no better than the opposite view of Johnson and Dover Wilson that Part 1, though it ends in Hotspur's death and the Prince's glory, is yet only the first half of a play. If it were a question of what Shakespeare intended in the matter, the evidence provided by what he wrote would not suggest either that the two parts were planned as a single drama or that Part 2 was an "unpremeditated sequel."

An escape from this dilemma has sometimes been sought in a theory, expounded especially by Professor Dover Wilson and Dr Tillyard, that what *Henry IV* shows is one action with two phases. While the whole drama shows the transformation of the madcap youth into the virtuous ruler, the first part, we are told, deals with the chivalric virtues, the second with the civil. In the first part the hero acquires honour, in the second he establishes justice. But I see no solution of the structural problem here. For though it is left to Part 2 to embody the idea of justice in the upright judge, the interest in justice and law is present from the start. On Falstaff's first appearance in Part 1 he jibes at the law as "old father antic." And he goes further. Included within his bubble is a vision of his future self not simply as a man freed from "the rusty curb" of the law but as a man who actually administers the law himself. "By the Lord, I'll be a brave judge," he says, making a mistake about his destined office which provokes Hal's retort, "Thou judgest false already." It is in the last act of Part 2 that we have the completion of this motif. Its climax comes when on Hal's accession Falstaff brags, "The laws of England are at my commandment," and its resolution when the true judge sends the false judge off to prison. But it begins, we see, in the first act of Part 1. The Prince's achievement in justice cannot, then, be regarded simply as the second phase of his progress. Certainly he has two contests: in one he outstrips Hotspur, in the other he puts down Falstaff. But these contests are not distributed at the rate of one per part. The plain fact is that in *Henry IV* two actions, each with the Prince as hero, begin together in the first act of Part 1, though one of them ends with the death of Hotspur at the end of Part 1, the other with the banishment of Falstaff at the end of Part 2.

Now, since the Falstaff plot is to take twice as long to complete its course, it might well be expected to develop from the beginning more slowly than the other. Certainly if it is to keep symmetry, it must come later to its turning-point. But is this in fact what we find? Frankly it is not. On the contrary, through the first half of Part 1 the Hotspur plot and the Falstaff plot show every sign of moving towards their crisis together.

Both plots, for example, are presented though I think both are not usually observed in the Prince's soliloquy in the first act which I have already quoted as foretelling the banishment of his tavern companions.

It is unfortunate that this speech has usually been studied for its bearing on Falstaff's rejection; its emphasis is really elsewhere. It is only the first two lines, with the reference to the "unyoked humour" of the Prince's companions, that allude specifically to them, and what is primarily in question is not what is to happen to the companions but what is to happen to the Prince. In the splendid image which follows of the sun breaking through the clouds we recognize a royal emblem and behold the promise of a radiant king who is to come forth from the "ugly mists" which at present obscure the Prince's real self. Since Falstaff has just been rejoicing at the thought that they "go by the moon . . . and not by Phœbus," it is apparent that his fortunes will decline when the Prince emerges like Phœbus himself. It is equally apparent, or should be, that the brilliant Hotspur will be outshone.[14] There is certainly no clue at this stage that the catastrophes of Hotspur and Falstaff will not be simultaneous.

Our expectation that they will be is indeed encouraged as the two actions now move forward. While Hotspur in pursuit of honour is preparing war, Falstaff displays his cowardice (I use the word advisedly) at Gadshill. While Hotspur rides forth from home on the journey that will take him to his downfall, the exposure of Falstaff's makebelieve in the matter of the men in buckram is the foreshadowing of his. The news of Hotspur's rebellion brings the Falstaffian revels to a climax at the same time as it summons the Prince to that interview with his father which will prove, as we have seen, the crisis of his career and the "nodal point" of the drama. That this interview is to be dramatically momentous is clear enough in advance: before we come to it, it is twice prefigured by the Prince and Falstaff in burlesque. But not only do the two mock-interviews excite our interest in the real one to come; the mock-interviews are in the story of the Prince and Falstaff what the real interview is in the story of the Prince and Hotspur. First, Falstaff, whose dream it is that he may one day govern England, basks in the makebelieve that he is king; and then Hal, who, as we have so often been reminded, is presently to be king, performs in masquerade his future part. The question they discuss is central to the play: "Shall the son of England prove a thief and take purses?" Shall he in fact continue to associate with Falstaff? One should notice that although the two actors exchange roles, they do not really change sides in this debate. Whether he acts the part of king or prince, Falstaff takes the opportunity of pleading for himself. When he is king he instructs the prince to "keep with" Falstaff; as prince he begs, "Banish not him thy Harry's company, banish not him thy Harry's company: banish plump Jack,

[14] *I.e.* This first-act soliloquy looks forward not only to the rejection of Falstaff but also to Vernon's vision of the Prince and his company before Shrewsbury, "gorgeous as the sun at midsummer."

and banish all the world." Falstaff's relations to the future king, a theme of speculation since the opening of the play, now come to a focus in this repeated word "banish." And when the Prince replies, "I do, I will," he anticipates in jest the sentence he is later to pronounce in earnest. If it were never to be pronounced in earnest, that would rob the masquerade of the dramatic irony from which comes its bouquet: those who accept Part 1 as a play complete in itself wrongly surrender their legitimate expectations. In this mock-interview the Prince declares his intentions towards Falstaff just as surely as in his real interview with his father he declares his intentions towards Hotspur. One declaration is a solemn vow, the other a glorious piece of fun, but they are equally prophetic and structurally their function is the same. We now approach the turning-point not of one, but of both dramatic actions. Indeed we miss the core of the play if we do not perceive that the two actions are really the same. The moment at the end of the third act when the Prince goes off to challenge Hotspur is also the moment when he leaves Falstaff's favourite tavern for what we well might think would be evermore. It is at the exit from the tavern that the road to Shrewsbury begins; and all the signposts I see indicate one-way traffic only. There should be no return.

The various dooms of Hotspur and Falstaff are now in sight; and we reasonably expect both dooms to be arrived at in Act 5. What we are not at all prepared for is that one of the two will be deferred till five acts later than the other. The symmetry so beautifully preserved in the story of Hotspur is in Falstaff's case abandoned. Statistics are known to be misleading, and nowhere more so than in literary criticism; but it is not without significance that in *Henry IV* Part 1 Falstaff's speeches in the first two acts number ninety-six and in the last two acts only twenty-five. As for Falstaff's satellites, with the exception of a single perfunctory appearance on the part of Bardolph, the whole galaxy vanishes altogether in the last two acts, only to reappear with some changes in personnel in Part 2. Falstaff, admittedly, goes on without a break, if broken in wind; and his diminished role does show some trace of the expected pattern of development. His going to war on foot while Hal is on horseback marks a separation of these erstwhile companions and a decline in Falstaff's status which was anticipated in jest when his horse was taken from him at Gadshill. When he nevertheless appears at one council of war his sole attempt at a characteristic joke is cut short by the Prince with "Peace, chewet, peace!" A fine touch, this, which contributes to the picture of the Prince's transformation: the boon companion whose jests he has delighted in is now silenced in a word. There is even the shadow of a rejection of Falstaff; over his supposed corpse the Prince speaks words that, for all their affectionate regret, remind us that he has turned his back on "vanity." But these things, however

significant, are details, no more than shorthand notes for the degrada-
tion of Falstaff that we have so confidently looked for. What it comes
to is that after the middle of Part 1 *Henry IV* changes its shape. And
that, it seems to me, is the root and cause of the structural problem.

Now that this change of shape has been, I hope I may say, demonstrated from within the play itself, it may at this stage be permissible
to venture an opinion about the author's plan. I do not of course mean
to imply that *Henry IV,* or indeed any other of Shakespeare's plays, ever
had a plan precisely laid down for it in advance. But it has to be supposed that when Shakespeare began a play he had some idea of the
general direction it would take, however ready he may have been to
modify his idea as art or expediency might suggest. Though this is
where I shall be told I pass the bounds of literary criticism into the
province of biography or worse, I hold it reasonable to infer from the
analysis I have given that in the course of writing *Henry IV* Shakespeare
changed his mind. I am compelled to believe that the author himself
foresaw, I will even say intended, that pattern which evolves through the
early acts of Part 1 and which demands for its completion that the hero's
rise to an eminence of valour shall be accompanied, or at least swiftly
followed, by the banishment of the riotous friends who hope to profit
from his reign. In other words, hard upon the Battle of Shrewsbury
there was to come the coronation of the hero as king. This inference
from the play is not without support from other evidence. The prince's
penitence in the interview with his father in the middle of Part 1 cor-
responds to an episode which, both in Holinshed and in the play of
The Famous Victories of Henry the Fifth, is placed only shortly before
the old king's death. And still more remarkable is the sequence of events
in a poem which has been shown to be one of Shakespeare's sources.[15]
At the historical Battle of Shrewsbury the Prince was only sixteen years
old, whereas Hotspur was thirty-nine. But in Samuel Daniel's poem,
The Civil Wars, Hotspur is made "young" and "rash" and encounters a
prince of equal age who emerges like a "new-appearing glorious star."[16]
It is Daniel, that is to say, who sets in opposition these two splendid
youths and so provides the germ from which grows the rivalry of the
Prince and Hotspur which is structural to Shakespeare's play. And in
view of this resemblance between Daniel and Shakespeare, it is significant that Daniel ignores the ten years that in history elapsed between
the death of Hotspur and the Prince's accession. Whereas in Holinshed
the events of those ten years fill nearly twenty pages, Daniel goes
straight from Shrewsbury to the old king's deathbed. This telescoping
of events, which confronts the Prince with his kingly responsibilities

15 See F. W. Moorman, "Shakespeare's History Plays and Daniel's 'Civile Wars,' " *Shakespeare Jahrbuch,* XL (1904), 77–83.
16 Book III, stanzas 97, 109–10.

directly after the slaying of Hotspur, adumbrates the pattern that Shakespeare, as I see it, must have had it in mind to follow out. The progress of a prince was to be presented not in two phases but in a single play of normal length which would show the hero wayward in its first half, pledging reform in the middle, and then in the second half climbing at Shrewsbury the ladder of honour by which, appropriately, he would ascend to the throne.

The exact point at which a new pattern supervenes I should not care to define. But I think the new pattern can be seen emerging during the fourth act. At a corresponding stage the history play of *Richard II* shows the deposition of its king, *Henry V* the victory at Agincourt, even *Henry IV* Part 2 the quelling of its rebellion in Gaultree Forest. By contrast *Henry IV* Part 1, postponing any such decisive action, is content with preparation. While the rebels gather, the Prince is arming and Falstaff recruiting to meet them. Until well into the fifth act ambassadors are going back and forth between the rival camps, and we may even hear a message twice over, once when it is despatched and once when it is delivered. True, this is not undramatic: these scenes achieve a fine animation and suspense as well as the lowlier feat of verisimilitude. But the technique is obviously not one of compression. Any thought of crowding into the two-hour traffic of one play the death of the old king and the coronation of the new has by now been relinquished, and instead the Battle of Shrewsbury is being built up into a grand finale in its own right. In our eagerness to come to this battle and our gratification at the exciting climax it provides, we easily lose sight of our previous expectations. Most of us, I suspect, go from the theatre well satisfied with the improvised conclusion. It is not, of course, that we cease to care about the fate of individuals. On the contrary, the battle succeeds so well because amid the crowded tumult of the fighting it keeps the key figures in due prominence. Clearly showing who is killed, who is rescued, and who shams dead, who slays a valiant foe and who only pretends to, it brings each man to a destiny that we perceive to be appropriate. We merely fail to notice that the destiny is not in every case exactly what was promised. There is no room now in Part 1 to banish Falstaff. A superb comic tact permits him instead the fate of reformation, in fact the alternative of giving over instead of being damned. It is a melancholy fate enough, for it means giving over being Falstaff: we leave him saying that if he is rewarded, he will "leave sack, and live cleanly as a nobleman should do." But since this resolution is conditional and need in any case be believed no more than Falstaff has already taught us to believe him, it has the advantage that it leaves the issue open, which, to judge from the outcry there has always been over the ending of Part 2, is how most people would prefer to have it left. Shakespeare's brilliant improvisation thus provides a dénouement to

Part 1 which has proved perfectly acceptable, while it still leaves opportunity for what I hope I may call the original ending, if the dramatist
should choose to add a second part. I refrain, however, from assuming
that a second part was necessarily planned before Part 1 was acted.

Part 2 itself does not require extended treatment. For whenever it
was "planned," it is a consequence of Part 1. Its freedom is limited by
the need to present what Part 1 so plainly prepared for and then left out.
Falstaff cannot be allowed to escape a second time. His opposition to
the law, being now the dominant interest, accordingly shapes the plot;
and the law, now bodied forth in the half-legendary figure of the Lord
Chief Justice, becomes a formidable person in the drama. The opening
encounter between these two, in which Falstaff makes believe not to see
or hear his reprover, is symbolic of Falstaff's whole attitude to law—he
ignores its existence as long as he can. But the voice which he at first
refuses to hear is the voice which will pronounce his final sentence. The
theme of the individual versus the law proves so fertile that it readily
gives rise to subplots. Justice Shallow, of course, claims his place in the
play by virtue of the life that is in him, exuberant in the capers of
senility itself. He functions all the same as the Lord Chief Justice's
antithesis: he is the foolish justice with whom Falstaff has his way and
from whom he wrings the thousand pounds that the wise justice has
denied him. Even Shallow's servant Davy has his relation to the law;
and his view of law is that though a man may be a knave, if he is my
friend and I am the justice's servant, it is hard if the knave cannot win.
In this humane sentiment Davy takes on full vitality as a person; but
he simultaneously brings us back to confront at a different angle the
main moral issue of the play. Is he to control the law or the law him?
In fact, shall Falstaff flourish or shall a thief be hanged?

It has sometimes been objected that Falstaff runs away with Part 2.
In truth he has to shoulder the burden of it because a dead man and a
converted one can give him small assistance. Part 2 has less opportunity for the integrated double action of Part 1. To be sure, it attempts
a double action, and has often been observed to be in some respects a
close replica of Part 1—"almost a carbon copy," Professor Shaaber says.
At exactly the same point in each part, for example, is a little domestic
scene where a rebel leader contemplates leaving home, and in each part
this is directly followed by the big tavern scene in which revelry rises
to a climax. And so on. An article in a recent number of *The Review
of English Studies* has even called *Henry IV* a diptych, finding the
"parallel presentation of incidents" in the two parts the primary formal
feature. I do not wish to deny the aesthetic satisfaction to be got from
a recognition of this rhythmic repetition; yet it is only the more super-
ficial pattern that can be thus repeated. With history and Holinshed
obliging, rebellion can break out as before; yet the rebellion of Part 2,

though it occupies our attention, has no significance, nor can have, for the principal characters of the play. The story of the Prince and Hotspur is over, and the King has only to die.

The one thing about history is that it does not repeat itself. Hotspur, unlike Sherlock Holmes, cannot come back to life. But there are degrees in all things; conversion has not quite the same finality as death. And besides, there is a type of hero whose adventures always can recur. Robin Hood has no sooner plundered one rich man than another comes along. It is the nature of Brer Fox, and indeed of Dr Watson, to be incapable of learning from experience. In folk-lore, that is to say, though not in history, you can be at the same point twice. And it seems as if Prince Hal may be sufficient of a folk-lore hero to be permitted to go again through the cycle of riot and reform. In Part 2 as in Part 1 the King laments his son's unprincely life. Yet this folk-lore hero is also a historical, and what is more to the point, a dramatic personage, and it is not tolerable that the victor of Shrewsbury should do as critics sometimes say he does, relapse into his former wildness and then reform again. The Prince cannot come into Part 2 unreclaimed without destroying the dramatic effect of Part 1. Yet if Part 2 is not to forgo its own dramatic effect, and especially its splendid last-act peripeteia, it requires a prince who is unreclaimed. This is Part 2's dilemma, and the way that it takes out of it is a bold one. When the King on his deathbed exclaims against the Prince's "headstrong riot," he has not forgotten that at Shrewsbury he congratulated the Prince on his redemption. He has not forgotten it for the simple reason that it has never taken place. The only man at court who believes in the Prince's reformation, the Earl of Warwick, believes that it will happen, not that it has happened already. Even as we watch the hero repeating his folk-lore cycle, we are positively instructed that he has not been here before:

> *The tide of blood in me*
> *Hath proudly flow'd in vanity till now.*

In the two parts of *Henry IV* there are not two princely reformations but two versions of a single reformation. And they are mutually exclusive. Though Part 2 frequently recalls and sometimes depends on what has happened in Part 1, it also denies that Part 1 exists. Accordingly the ideal spectator of either part must not cry with Shakespeare's Lucio, "I know what I know." He must sometimes remember what he knows and sometimes be content to forget it. This, however, is a requirement made in some degree by any work of fiction, or as they used to call it, feigning. And the feat is not a difficult one for those accustomed to grant the poet's demand for "that willing suspension of disbelief . . . which constitutes poetic faith."

Henry IV, then, is both one play and two. Part 1 begins an action which it finds it has not scope for but which Part 2 rounds off. But with one half of the action already concluded in Part 1, there is danger of a gap in Part 2. To stop the gap Part 2 expands the unfinished story of Falstaff and reduplicates what is already finished in the story of the Prince. The two parts are complementary, they are also independent and even incompatible. What they are, with their various formal anomalies, I suppose them to have become through what Johnson termed "the necessity of exhibition." Though it would be dangerous to dispute Coleridge's view that a work of art must "contain in itself the reason why it is so," that its form must proceed from within,[17] yet even works of art, like other of man's productions, must submit to the bondage of the finite. . . .

[17] This is a synthesis of several passages in Coleridge. The words in quotation marks are said of whatever can give permanent pleasure; but the context shows Coleridge to be thinking of literary composition. See *Biographia Literaria*, ed. Shawcross, ii. 9. Also relevant are "On Poesy or Art," *ibid.*, ii. 262; and *Coleridge's Shakespearean Criticism*, ed. T. M. Raysor, i. 223–4.

CLIFFORD LEECH

The Unity of 2 Henry IV[1]

IT SHOULD perhaps be made clear that this is not a contribution to the debate on Shakespeare's original planning of the Prince Henry plays. It has been argued by Dover Wilson in *The Fortunes of Falstaff* and in his New Cambridge edition, and by E. M. W. Tillyard in *Shakespeare's History Plays,* that the two parts of *Henry IV* constitute one long play, envisaged at least in its main outlines from the very beginning of Part I. M. A. Shaaber, on the other hand, has put a case for regarding Part II as a sequel, outside Shakespeare's original plan, brought into being through the remarkable success of Part I.[2] Whichever of these views is correct, it is possible for Part II to have its own characteristic mood and structure, its separate dramatic impact, and my concern will be to demonstrate that this is indeed the case. The only assumption I shall make, which I think will be readily granted to me, is that Part II was written after Part I.

In writing the series of eight plays which give an outline of English history from the reign of Richard II to the accession of Henry VII, Shakespeare can hardly at the beginning have seen the scheme as a whole. If he had, it would be odd to start with the troubles of Henry VI. The mention of Prince Henry near the end of *Richard II* suggests it was then that Shakespeare began to think of plays in which he would be the central figure, plays which would close the gap between Boling-broke's usurpation and the funeral of Henry V. But clearly the plays in the sequence already written had been markedly different from one another in structure and atmosphere. This was partly, of course, because

From *Shakespeare Survey 6,* ed. A. Nicoll (Cambridge, 1953), pp. 16–24. Reprinted by permission of Cambridge University Press and of the author.

[1] This article is based on a paper read at the Shakespeare Conference, Stratford-upon-Avon, in August 1951.
[2] "The Unity of *Henry IV,*" *Joseph Quincy Adams Memorial Studies,* 1948, pp. 217–27. Since this article was written, H. Edward Cain has supported Shaaber's case in "Further Light on the Relation of *1* and *2 Henry IV,*" *Shakespeare Quarterly,* III (January 1952), 21–38.

Shakespeare's grasp of play-making and dramatic language was rapidly becoming more secure, but partly too it was because the action of each play had demanded a specific handling. There are recognizable distinctions in material and manner between the three *Henry VI* plays, and when Shakespeare continued the story with *Richard III* he employed a new massiveness and formality of structure in his presentation of a strong man who abused his sovereign power in the wanton exercise of his own will: Richard of Gloucester, the Samson in the devil's cause who brought down the temple upon himself, demanded a play in which all his followers and adversaries were reduced almost to a choric function, until Henry of Richmond came, as a god from over sea, to confront him. The play of *Richard II,* because Shakespeare saw the King as a man too conceited for scruple, complacent in his royalty, and yet with an exquisite taste in suffering, had necessarily a quieter tone, a more human presentation of the usurper, an elegiac note because this play marked the beginning of England's trouble. So, later on, with *Henry V,* the glorious interlude which had its centre in Agincourt was to be punctuated only with marks of exclamation, those chorus-passages directed at keeping the mind alight: the only conflict was that of arms, and for once it is not the sickness of the commonwealth that we are asked to consider, but the success of a foreign campaign. In describing these plays, I have of course simplified their effects. There are quieter, elegiac moments even in the grim ritual of *Richard III;* national glory is for a little, when Gaunt dies, the theme of *Richard II;* and there are passages in *Henry V* which demonstrate that the strife and intrigue of the previous reign are by no means done. Yet there is a dominant tone in each drama. Similarly, each of the two parts of *Henry IV* makes its characteristic and distinct impression on us.

When Shakespeare began to write of the youth of Prince Henry, he had indeed a subject that called for lightness of heart. Here was a young man, having his fun, yet not compromising himself so far that he could not later shine in council and on the field of battle. The civil troubles of his usurping father could not be shirked, but at least these troubles were manageable and might even afford some apprenticeship for the growing Prince. Coleridge has described *Romeo and Juliet* as a play given unity of feeling by the youth and springtime that permeate every character and moment: even its old men, he says, have "an eagerness, a hastiness, a precipitancy—the effect of spring."[3] That might almost be our judgement too of *1 Henry IV*. There is a graver note in the portraits of the King and old Northumberland, but the dominant feeling is young, excited, good-hearted. The Prince must not forget his future, must not think exclusively in terms of personal glory, as Hotspur does,

[3] *Coleridge's Shakespearean Criticism* (ed. Raysor, 1930), II, 265.

must not think only of the moment's pleasure, as Falstaff does: but he can and should value these things, while recognizing their subordination to the obligations and opportunities that will come to him with the golden round. When seeing Part I, we may prefer the company of either Hotspur or Falstaff to that of the Prince, but we are not out of sympathy with him, and esteem him when he shows respect for Hotspur and liking for Falstaff. At the end of Part I, he has overcome Hotspur in single combat, an incident not found in Holinshed: he has revealed himself as the good and honourable fighter needed for the play of Agincourt.

In arguing that Part II was an "unpremeditated addition," which need not concern us here, R. A. Law[4] has emphasized the morality characteristics of that Part, the placing of Prince Henry between the personified representations of order (in the Lord Chief Justice) and disorder (in Falstaff). This account of the play's structure has been elaborated by Tillyard, though of course he disagrees with Law on the play's origin. It does indeed now seem beyond question that the Prince, no longer on the field of battle, is exhibited as slowly abandoning his old associations with disorder and becoming ultimately at one with its opposite. Not that we have a "conversion," as in the old moralities, but rather a manifestation of a hitherto concealed adherence. This part of the play's substance becomes most noticeable towards its end, when Falstaff is ready to steal any man's horses because his "dear boy" is on the throne, and Doll and the Hostess are taken to prison for being concerned in a man's death. To demonstrate this second phase in Hal's apprenticeship is the overt intention of this Part, as we may say that the overt intention of *Macbeth* is to demonstrate the ills that come upon a man and his country when he murders his King and steals the crown. But just as we may think that there is a secondary intention to *Macbeth*, to hint at a protest against the very frame of things, so in this Second Part of *Henry IV* we may feel that the dramatist, in giving us the preparation for Agincourt, hints also at a state of dubiety concerning basic assumptions in the great historical scheme. He shows us the new King adhering to political order, yet makes us half-doubt whether that order is worth its price, whether in fact it is of the deepest importance to men. And with this element of doubt, the poet's awareness of mutability grows more intense.

Whether Part II was a new play or a continuation of one already begun, the battle of Shrewsbury had marked the end of a phase. Shakespeare, returning to his subject, and to a more sober aspect of that subject (for law has not the manifest attractiveness of chivalrous encounter), was bound to approach his task with less light-heartedness, with a cooler and more objective view. Just as Marlowe in *Tamburlaine* ap-

[4] "Structural Unity in the Two Parts of *Henry the Fourth*," *Studies in Philology*, xxiv (1927), 223–42.

pears to see his hero with less enthusiasm in Part II than in Part I, recognizing his excess as such and not keeping him immune from ridicule, so here Shakespeare weighs his characters more carefully and questions even the accuracy of his balance.

This note in the play is, I think, struck in the Induction itself. Clearly Shakespeare needed an introductory speech here, both to remind his auditors of what had happened at Shrewsbury and to make plain the irony of the false news brought to Northumberland in the first scene of the play. But he is not content with a simple Prologue. His speaker is a quasi-morality figure, and no pleasant one. Rumour expresses scorn for the credulity of men, and even—though irrelevantly—for their love of slander. The scorn is brought home when Rumour calls the audience he addresses "my household." In tone this Induction is similar to the Prologue to *Troilus and Cressida:* there too the speaker was in a costume appropriate to the mood of the play—"A Prologue arm'd . . . suited in like conditions as our argument"—and there too the tone was not gentle.

In the play we at once meet Northumberland, who has not gained much of our affection in either of the two earlier plays in which he appeared. Here he is the first of a series of old and sick men that we are to encounter. Falstaff and Justice Shallow, King Henry IV and the Lord Chief Justice, are all burdened with their years, and the only one in full command of his wits and his body is the character given no personal name and conceived almost as a morality-presentment of the Justice which he executes. Dover Wilson has drawn our attention to the way in which our attitude to Falstaff is made to change in the course of this Second Part,[5] though in concentrating on the figures of Prince Hal and the Knight he does not perhaps fully relate this change to the new atmosphere in the drama as a whole. When we first meet Falstaff in I, ii, his talk is at once of his diseases, and he reverts to this at the end of the scene when, like Ancient Pistol in *Henry V,* he asserts his readiness to "turn diseases to commodity." There is, of course, plenty of gaiety in his talk of disease, as there is in the scene with Doll at the Boar's Head: we delight in the comedy of it, but the frailty of ageing flesh is grotesque as well as amusing. Before we see "Saturn and Venus in conjunction," we are told by the Drawers of how Falstaff was once "anger'd . . . to the heart" when the Prince jested rudely on his age. The comedy here and in Gloucestershire has a sharper savour because we are never allowed to forget the evidence of decay. Justice Shallow, wrapping his thin frame in a fanciful tapestry of wild youth, is comedy of the rarest sort, but "Jesu, the days that we have seen!" is a line with a barb in it for us all. And the King, in his different way, belongs with these men. When we first meet him in Act III, he is longing for the

---

[5] *The Fortunes of Falstaff* (1943), pp. 93–8.

sleep denied him; he cannot rid himself of guilt, ever more and more pathetically he talks of the crusade he will never make; and when he is dying he asks to be carried to the chamber called Jerusalem, so that the prophecy may be fulfilled and he may derive consolation from submitting to what has been decreed.

Along with the Falstaff scenes and the scenes at court, we have other parts of this play where a rebellion is launched and destroyed. This enterprise is contrasted sharply with the rebellion in Part I. There is no Hotspur to give dash and gaiety to it. His father is once more "crafty-sick," and the leadership of the revolt is in the grave hands of the Archbishop of York. He is not presented as a man scheming for advancement but as one who gives a measure of sanctification to the rebels' cause. Yet when they come together for the planning of their campaign, their language is hesitant, cautious, argumentative, as if they would talk themselves out of a situation from which there is no escape. At the end of i, i there is little hope in Northumberland's voice as he bids

> Get posts and letters, and make friends with speed:
> Never so few, and never yet more need.

And Hastings's concluding cry in i, iii—"We are time's subjects, and time bids, be gone"—has a fatalistic ring. It is no surprise to us when Northumberland's defection is shown, and it seems appropriate that these rebels, so given to sober talk, should be vanquished by a verbal trick before a blow is exchanged. In Holinshed it is not Prince John of Lancaster but the Earl of Westmoreland who dupes the rebels:[6] Shakespeare uses Westmoreland as an ambassador of Prince John, but gives to the King's son all the doubtful credit of the action. The change can, I think, only be explained by the assumption that Shakespeare wanted to bring this line of conduct more closely home to the royal house. Because Prince John is the King's son and Hal's brother, the stain of the exploit falls partly on them. Perhaps some will claim that such conduct was justified in the cause of law and order, that an Elizabethan would simply admire the skill of it. Yet is it possible not to find irony in John's concluding speech in the scene of Gaultree Forest?

> I promised you redress of these same grievances
> Whereof you did complain; which, by mine honour,
> I will perform with a most Christian care.   (iv, ii, 113–15)

In the mouth of the astute Prince John the word "Christian" has an effect gross and palpable. When he proceeds to claim "God, and not we, hath safely fought to-day," we seem to recognize blasphemy. If this is not plain enough, one can turn to the next scene, where Falstaff demands

[6] *The Historie of England* (1587), iii, 529–30.

from Prince John recompense for taking Sir John Colevile prisoner: he will otherwise, he says, see to his own glorification in ballad and picture: if that does not come to pass, he tells Prince John to "believe not the word of the noble." A few lines before we have seen the value of a noble's word in Gaultree Forest, and there is therefore strong irony in Falstaff thus exhorting Prince John. Nor should we overlook Shakespeare's reminder that Prince John's adroit handling of the situation is but a momentary trick. Hastings has told him that, if this revolt is put down, others will rise against the House of Lancaster:

> And though we here fall down,
> We have supplies to second our attempt:
> If they miscarry, theirs shall second them;
> And so success of mischief shall be born,
> And heir from heir shall hold this quarrel up,
> Whiles England shall have generation. (iv, ii, 44–9)

To that John replies:

> You are too shallow, Hastings, much too shallow,
> To sound the bottom of the after-times.

It is Hastings who is right: John is too vain to see the total situation.

I have said that Shakespeare's substitution of Prince John for Westmoreland in the Gaultree affair brings the taint of it nearer to the King and Hal. When the play ends, and the new King has banished his old followers, the stage is empty except for Prince John and the Lord Chief Justice. Before mentioning the talk of French wars, Prince John spares a moment to praise his brother: "I like this fair proceeding of the king's," he says. It is surely not enviable to be praised by such men as Prince John. It is like Flamineo in *The White Devil* praising Brachiano's hypocritical display of grief for Isabella's death. Praise like that is a burden for a man to carry. We need not dispute that it was necessary to banish Falstaff if England was to be for a time secure and Agincourt won. But we are made to realize that there is a heavy price to pay for political success. Indeed, we are reminded of it in the succeeding play, when, during the battle itself, Fluellen refers to the rejection of the fat knight whose name he has forgotten.

In Shakespearian drama there is often a condition of tension between the play's overt meaning and its deeper implications. The gaiety of *Twelfth Night* is enriched by the thread of sadness that runs through it, but we cannot say that the baiting of Malvolio is in easy accord with the play's surface texture. In *Macbeth* the enfolding of the tragic idea within a morality pattern leaves us with a feeling of suspended judgement in which we resent Malcolm's concluding reference to "this dead butcher, and his fiend-like queen." So in this Second Part of *Henry IV* the deeper, more disturbing implications impinge directly on the main action of the drama, and then, as in *Macbeth*, the writer appears to strain for the re-establishment of the original framework. We get this feeling in the harshness of the words that Henry V uses to Falstaff, for we have come to wonder a little whether there is ultimately much to choose between Falstaff and Prince John, and indeed we greatly prefer Falstaff's company. And the same feeling emerges, I think, in the often praised scene where Hal is reconciled to his father. Justifying his taking of the crown when he believed his father dead, he says:

> I spake unto this crown as having sense
> And thus upbraided it: 'The care on thee depending,
> Hath fed upon the body of my father;
> Therefore, thou best of gold art worst of gold.
> Other, less fine in carat, is more precious,
> Preserving life in medicine potable:
> But thou, most fine, most honour'd, most renown'd,
> Hast eat thy bearer up.' Thus, my most royal liege,
> Accusing it, I put it on my head,
> To try with it, as with an enemy
> That had before my face murder'd my father,
> The quarrel of a true inheritor.   (IV, v, 158–69)

The elaborateness of the imagery is notable: the burden of the crown is a devouring monster, its gold is contrasted to *aurum potabile*, it is a murderer with whom the dead man's son must wage a blood-feud. In this scene and in the new King's rejection of Falstaff, the note of sternness and sobriety is heavily, almost clumsily, pressed down, in an attempt to silence the basic questions that so often in the play demand to be put. And perhaps, when he had done, Shakespeare realized that this close was altogether too ponderous for a play that had taken us to the Boar's Head and into Gloucestershire, and altogether too assured for a play persistently though not obtrusively concerned with change and ineradicable frailty. So he gave us the dancer's epilogue, in tripping prose, with its casual half-promise that Falstaff would come again in the next play: the banishment was to be merely from the King, and not from us. Later he was to change his mind again, perhaps because he realized that Sir John was no longer a figure of delight: around him had grown a small forest of disturbing thoughts, which might well choke the brief glory of Agincourt. *Henry V* was not the climax of a series, but rather an interlude, a holiday-play, in which for a while disaster was kept remote. Its epilogue does make plain that by this time Shakespeare had come to see his eight-play sequence as a whole, and within that sequence the Agincourt play must be predominantly sun-lit. He had to avoid, not too much gaiety with Falstaff, but too little. It is all the more remarkable that the questioning mood of *2 Henry IV* does show itself here and there in the succeeding play—with the intrigues of Canterbury and Ely; the frank presentation of many unchivalrous details of the war, from Bardolph's stealing of a "pax" to the King's twice-given order that every man shall kill his prisoners; the repeated reminder that a war-maker must have a just cause. But these things on the whole are kept in their place, and an audience for *Henry V* is not much disturbed in its dream of glory. In *2 Henry IV*, on the other hand, an audience is rarely at its ease.

In Law's paper on *Henry IV*, to which I have already acknowledged a debt, the darker side of Part II is in no way brought out. But Law does draw attention to the comic echoing of serious things in the play: Henry IV's sick memories of his early life are immediately followed, he points out, by Justice Shallow's maunderings on his deeds in the same period; Davy's petition to Shallow that "a knave should have some countenance at his friend's request" reminds us of Prince Hal's vigorous intercession for Bardolph with the Lord Chief Justice. There are a number of other ironic echoes in the play. At the end of the Boar's Head scene, when "a dozen captains" come to summon Falstaff to court, the Knight rises to the occasion, putting his rest from him:

> Pay the musicians, sirrah. Farewell Hostess; farewell Doll. You see, my good wenches, how men of merit are sought after: the undeserver may sleep, when the man of action is called on.   (ii, iv, 403–6)

It is immediately after this that Henry IV has his famous utterance on the sleeplessness of kings. We are the less inclined to contemplate the ills of greatness with awe, because Falstaff has taken them to himself already. We have noted the way in which Falstaff's "believe not the word of the noble" comes immediately after the scene in Gaultree Forest, but in iii, ii there is an echo at Falstaff's expense. In Part I he has this exchange with the Prince when the battle of Shrewsbury is about to begin:

> *Fal.*   I would 'twere bed-time, Hal, and all well.
> *Prince*   Why, thou owest God a death.
> *Fal.*   'Tis not due yet; I would be loath to pay him
> before his day.   (v, i, 125–9)

Then there follows the "catechism" on "Honour." In Part II the despised Feeble has a moment of splendour when, unlike Bullcalf and Mouldy, he does not attempt to escape from impressment:

> By my troth, I care not; a man can die but once: we owe God a death: I'll ne'er bear a base mind: an't be my destiny, so; an't be not, so: no man is too good to serve's prince: and let it go which way it will, he that dies this year is quit for the next.   (iii, ii, 250–5)

There is of course an absurdity in these words of bravery poured from so weak a vessel, yet they demand respect. Bardolph's reply, "Well said; thou'rt a good fellow," cannot be wholly ironic, and the impressiveness of the effect is only mitigated, not destroyed, when Feeble comes out again with his "Faith, I'll bear no base mind." The interplay of feelings in this Second Part is so complex that our sympathy resides securely nowhere. Falstaff can be used to direct our feelings, as he does with Prince John, and often through the play we prefer his gross and witty animality to the politic management of the Lancastrians. But just as the dramatist makes no attempt to disguise his age and sickness or even a churlish arrogance in him, so here he is put down by Feeble's curious, inverted echo of his own words in the First Part. I am of course not suggesting that Shakespeare could expect an audience to note the echo: for us, however, it seems to indicate a trend of feeling in the writer's mind.

The remarkable degree of objectivity in the presentation of the characters reminds us of certain later plays of Shakespeare, those that we call the "dark comedies." It is not merely through our latter-day squeamishness, I believe, that we are made uneasy by the presentation of the Duke and Isabella in *Measure for Measure;* and in *Troilus and Cressida* Shakespeare's own Prologue warns us that the expectation of armed strife is "tickling skittish spirits, On one and other side." And *2 Henry IV* is close to these plays also in the peculiarly acrid flavour of certain generalized utterances. On his first appearance in the play, the King sees the process of time in geological change and in the pattern of a human life, and there is no comfort in the vision, only a desire to have done:

> O God! that one might read the book of fate,
> And see the revolution of the times
> Make mountains level, and the continent,
> Weary of solid firmness, melt itself
> Into the sea! and, other times, to see
> The beachy girdle of the ocean
> Too wide for Neptune's hips; how chances mock
> And changes fill the cup of alteration
> With divers liquors! O, if this were seen,
> The happiest youth, viewing his progress through,
> What perils past, what crosses to ensue,
> Would shut the book, and sit him down and die. (III, i, 45–56)

And when he is himself dying and he believes that his son has greedily seized the crown in advance of his right, he speaks of the human greed for gold, a theme no Elizabethan could long avoid, and how each generation is impatient for possession:

> See, sons, what things you are!
> How quickly nature falls into revolt

When gold becomes her object!
For this the foolish over-careful fathers
Have broke their sleep with thoughts, their brains with care,
Their bones with industry;
For this they have engrossed and piled up
The canker'd heaps of strange-achieved gold;
For this they have been thoughtful to invest
Their sons with arts and martial exercises:
When, like the bee, culling from every flower
The virtuous sweets,
Our thighs pack'd with wax, our mouths with honey,
We bring it to the hive, and, like the bees,
Are murdered for our pains. This bitter taste
Yield his engrossments to the ending father.   (iv, v, 65–80)

This is not far from what the Duke has to say to the condemned
Claudio in *Measure for Measure*. Though he wears a friar's habit, he
gives no religious consolation, but bids him see the vanity of existence,
the impossibility of any sure possession, the cold impatience of an heir:

Friend hast thou none;
For thine own bowels, which do call thee sire,
The mere effusion of thy proper loins,
Do curse the gout, serpigo, and the rheum,
For ending thee no sooner.   (iii, i, 28–32)

It seems probable that *2 Henry IV* was written some three years before
Troilus, some six before *Measure for Measure*, yet here Shakespeare anticipates that objectivity of manner, fused with a suggestion of deep and
personal concern, which is characteristic of these two later plays. The
sequence of the histories depends on the cardinal assumption that order
in a commonwealth is a prime good: it is not altogether surprising that,
as his task came towards its conclusion, and with the additional effort
required in writing a second play on a young king's apprenticeship,
Shakespeare should have reached a condition of dubiety, should have
felt less secure in his assumptions. The "dark comedies" come during
the tragic period, and in their way give evidence of a similar slackening
of grasp. The basic assumption made by the tragic writer is that a
personal goodness, inexplicable and apparently futile, can nevertheless
be realized. But, unless the writer has the sense of a direct revelation,
this assumption can be maintained only by strong effort: in the "dark
comedies" the mind is not kept tragically taut.

So far from demonstrating "the unity of *2 Henry IV*," it may appear
that I have shown only a clash of feelings within the play, an overt
morality intention, a preoccupation with the effects of time, and a latent
scepticism. That I would acknowledge, while maintaining that such a
contradiction persists in all the major plays of the Elizabethan and

Jacobean years. The tragic figures of the time are of great stature, compelling our awe, but we are not spared realization that they can be petty and grotesque and villainous as well. They are made to seem free agents in their choice of good or evil, yet simultaneously we are made certain, from the beginning of the play, that destruction will be theirs. So, in the best comedy, the gay march from wooing to wedding, from pretence to its merry discomfiture, is counterpointed with a low murmur of regret. Elizabethan dramas are rich in implication because they have emotional, but not logical, coherence. We travel two roads, or more, at once. We arrive at no destination. But, home again once more, we feel that—if we could but speak effectively of such things—we should have travellers' tales to tell.

But it has been apparent, I think, that *2 Henry IV* differs from Part I in its dominant tone. Of course, there are sharp incidental things in the earlier play, but they do not weigh heavily on the spectator's mind. Falstaff abuses the press in both Parts, but his activities in this direction are shown at closer quarters in Part II. And there is broad merriment in the later play, but it is worked into a pattern where good humour is not the main theme. Towards the end of Part II there is, indeed, a strong measure of simplification. From the Prince's last interview with his father to the rejection of Falstaff, Shakespeare strives to make the morality-element all-pervading, until we have the curious spectacle of Henry V urging repentance on his old companions: banishment was, of course, required, but he is an odd preacher to men whom kingship did not call to the disciplined life. And, as we have seen, the prose epilogue pretends that, after all, merriment is the prime concern of this play and the one to come. But, until Henry IV's death-scene, the delicate balance between the two layers of meaning is skilfully maintained.

When one is interpreting a Shakespeare play, one is always in danger of being reminded that Shakespeare was an Elizabethan, that his assumptions and standards of judgement were therefore different from ours. Tillyard has commented thus on Prince Hal's treatment of Francis in Part I:

> The subhuman element in the population must have been considerable in Shakespeare's day; that it should be treated almost like beasts was taken for granted.[7]

But is not this to overlook the fact that Shakespeare can make us resent the ill-treatment of any human being, and respect the most insignificant of creatures, a Feeble or a servant of the Duke of Cornwall? In *Measure for Measure* he reminds us that even an insect shares with us the experience of death and corporal suffering. He was an Elizabethan certainly:

[7] *Shakespeare's History Plays* (1944), p. 277.

he made assumptions about kingship and "degree" and incest and adultery that perhaps we may not make. But he was also a human being with a remarkable degree of sensitivity: it is indeed for that reason that he can move us so much. If he merely had skill in "putting over" characteristic Tudor ideas, we could leave him to the social and political historians. Because his reaction to suffering, his esteem for good faith, his love of human society, his sense of mutability and loss, his obscure notion of human grandeur, his ultimate uncertainty of value, are not basically different from ours—though more deeply felt and incomparably expressed—he belongs supremely to literature. We do him, I think, scant justice if we assume that he could write complacently of Prince John of Lancaster, and could have no doubts about Prince Hal.

MAURICE MORGANN

Courage and the Character of Falstaff

. . . It is not to the *Courage* only of *Falstaff* that we think these observations will apply: No part whatever of his character seems to be fully settled in our minds; at least there is something strangely incongruous in our discourse and affections concerning him. We all like *Old Jack;* yet, by some strange perverse fate, we all abuse him, and deny him the possession of any one single good or respectable quality. There is something extraordinary in this: It must be a strange art in *Shakespeare* which can draw our liking and good will towards so offensive an object. He has wit, it will be said; chearfulness and humour of the most characteristic and captivating sort. And is this enough? Is the humour and gaiety of vice so very captivating? Is the wit, characteristic of baseness and every ill quality capable of attaching the heart and winning the affections? Or does not the apparency of such humour, and the flashes of such wit, by more strongly disclosing the deformity of character, but the more effectually excite our hatred and contempt of the man? And yet this is not our *feeling* of *Falstaff's* character. When he has ceased to amuse us, we find no emotions of disgust; we can scarcely forgive the ingratitude of the Prince in the new-born virtue of the King, and we curse the severity of that poetic justice which consigns our old good-natured delightful companion to the custody of the *warden,* and the dishonours of the *Fleet.*

I am willing, however, to admit that if a Dramatic writer will but preserve to any character the qualities of a strong mind, particularly Courage and ability, that it will be afterwards no very difficult task (as I may have occasion to explain) to discharge that *disgust* which arises from vicious manners; and even to attach us (if such character should contain any quality productive of chearfulness and laughter) to the cause and subject of our mirth with some degree of affection.

From "An Essay on the Dramatic Character of Sir John Falstaff" (1777), in *Shakespeare Criticism: A Selection,* ed. D. Nichol Smith (Oxford, 1916), pp. 153–189. Title supplied by the present editor. (The complete essay appears in D. Nichol Smith, *Eighteenth Century Essays on Shakespeare,* Oxford, 1903. It is discussed in the present volume by Stewart, Langbaum, and Sewell.)

But the question which I am to consider is of a very different nature: It is a question of fact, and concerning a quality which forms the basis of every respectable character; a quality which is the very essence of a Military man; and which is held up to us, in almost every Comic incident of the Play, as the subject of our observation. It is strange then that it should now be a question, whether *Falstaff* is, or is not a man of Courage; and whether we do in fact contemn him for the want, or respect him for the possession of that quality: And yet I believe the reader will find that he has by no means decided this question, even for himself.—If then it should turn out, that this difficulty has arisen out of the Art of *Shakespeare*, who has contrived to make secret Impressions upon us of Courage, and to preserve those Impressions in favour of a character which was to be held up for sport and laughter on account of actions of apparent Cowardice and dishonour, we shall have less occasion to wonder, as *Shakespeare* is a Name which contains All of Dramatic artifice and genius. . . .

To me then it appears that the leading quality in *Falstaff's* character, and that from which all the rest take their colour, is a high degree of wit and humour, accompanied with great natural vigour and alacrity of mind. This quality so accompanied, led him probably very early into life, and made him highly acceptable to society; so acceptable, as to make it seem unnecessary for him to acquire any other virtue. Hence, perhaps, his continued debaucheries and dissipations of every kind.—He seems, by nature, to have had a mind free of malice or any evil principle; but he never took the trouble of acquiring any good one. He found himself esteemed and beloved with all his faults; nay *for* his faults, which were all connected with humour, and for the most part, grew out of it. As he had, possibly, no vices but such as he thought might be openly professed, so he appeared more dissolute thro' ostentation. To the character of wit and humour, to which all his other qualities seem to have conformed themselves, he appears to have added a very necessary support, *that* of the profession of a *Soldier*. He had from nature, as I presume to say, a spirit of boldness and enterprise; which in a Military age, tho' employment was only occasional, kept him always above contempt, secured him an honourable reception among the Great, and suited best both with his particular mode of humour and of vice. Thus living continually in society, nay even in Taverns, and indulging himself, and being indulged by others, in every debauchery; drinking, whoring, gluttony, and ease; assuming a liberty of fiction, necessary perhaps to his wit, and often falling into falsity and lies, he seems to have set, by degrees, all sober reputation at defiance; and finding eternal resources in his wit, he borrows, shifts, defrauds, and even robs, without dishonour.—Laughter and approbation attend his greatest excesses; and being governed visibly by no settled bad principle or ill design, fun and humour account for and cover all. By degrees, however, and thro' indulgence, he acquires bad habits, becomes an humourist, grows enormously corpulent and falls into the infirmities of age; yet never quits, all the time, one single levity or vice of youth, or loses any of that chearfulness of mind, which had enabled him to pass thro' this course with ease to himself and delight to others; and thus, at last, mixing youth and age, enterprize and corpulency, wit and folly, poverty and expence, title and buffoonery, innocence as to purpose, and wickedness as to practice; neither incurring hatred by bad principle, or contempt by Cowardice, yet involved in circumstances productive of imputation in both; a butt and a wit, a humourist and a man of humour, a touchstone and a laughing stock, a jester and a jest, has Sir *John Falstaff*, taken at that period of his life in which we see him, become the most perfect Comic character that perhaps ever was exhibited.

It may not possibly be wholly amiss to remark in this place, that if Sir *John Falstaff* had possessed any of that Cardinal quality, Prudence, alike the guardian of virtue and the protector of vice; that quality, from the possession or the absence of which, the character and fate of men in this life take, I think, their colour, and not from real vice or virtue; if he had considered his wit not as *principal* but *accessary* only; as the instrument of power, and not as power itself; if he had had much baseness to hide, if he had had less of what may be called mellowness or good humour, or less of health and spirit; if he had spurred and rode the world with his wit, instead of suffering the world, boys and all, to ride him;—he might, without any other essential change, have been the admiration and not the jest of mankind:—Or if he had lived in our day, and instead of attaching himself to one Prince, had renounced *all* friendship and *all* attachment, and had let himself out as the ready instrument and Zany of every successive Minister, he might possibly have acquired the high honour of marking his shroud or decorating his coffin with the living rays of an Irish at least, if not a British Coronet: Instead of which, tho' enforcing laughter from every disposition, he appears, now, as such a character, which every wise man will pity and avoid, every knave will censure, and every fool will fear: And accordingly *Shakespeare*, ever true to nature, has made *Harry* desert, and *Lancaster* censure him:—He dies where he lived, in a Tavern, broken-hearted, without a friend; and his final exit is given up to the derision of fools. Nor have his misfortunes ended here; the scandal arising from the misapplication of his wit and talents seems immortal. He has met with as little justice or mercy from his final judges the critics, as from his companions of the Drama. With our cheeks still red with laughter, we ungratefully as unjustly censure him as a coward by nature, and a rascal upon principle: Tho', if this were so, it might be hoped, for our own credit, that we should behold him rather with disgust and disapprobation than with pleasure and delight. . . .

Tho' I have considered *Falstaff's* character as relative only to one single quality, yet so much has been said, that it cannot escape the reader's notice that he is a character made up by *Shakespeare* wholly of incongruities;—a man at once young and old, enterprizing and fat, a dupe and a wit, harmless and wicked, weak in principle and resolute by constitution, cowardly in appearance and brave in reality; a knave without malice, a lyar without deceit; and a knight, a gentleman, and a soldier, without either dignity, decency, or honour: This is a character, which, though it may be decompounded, could not, I believe, have been formed, nor the ingredients of it duly mingled upon any receipt whatever: It required the hand of *Shakespeare* himself to give to every particular part a relish of the whole, and of the whole to every particular part;—alike the same incongruous, identical *Falstaff*, whether to the grave Chief Justice he vainly talks of his youth, and offers to *caper for a thousand;* or cries to Mrs. *Doll, "I am old, I am old,"* though she is seated on his lap, and he is courting her for busses. How *Shakespeare* could furnish out sentiment of so extraordinary a composition, and supply it with such appropriated and characteristic language, humour and wit, I cannot tell; but I may, however, venture to infer, and that confidently, that he who so well understood the use of incongruity, and that laughter was to be raised by the opposition of qualities in the same man, and not by their agreement or conformity, would never have attempted to raise mirth by shewing us Cowardice in a Coward unattended by Pretence, and softened by every excuse of age, corpulence, and infirmity: And of this we cannot have a more striking proof than his furnishing this very character, on one instance of real terror, however excusable, with boast, braggadocio, and pretence, exceeding that of all other stage Cowards the whole length of his superior wit, humour, and invention.

What then upon the whole shall be said but that *Shakespeare* has made certain Impressions, or produced certain effects, of which he has thought fit to conceal or obscure the cause? How he has done this, and for what special ends, we shall now presume to guess.—Before the period in which *Shakespeare* wrote, the fools and Zanys of the stage were drawn out of the coarsest and cheapest materials: Some essential folly, with a dash of knave and coxcomb, did the feat. But *Shakespeare,* who delighted in difficulties, was resolved to furnish a richer repast, and to give to one eminent buffoon the high relish of wit, humour, birth, dignity, and Courage. But this was a process which required the nicest hand, and the utmost management and address: These enumerated qualities are, in their own nature, productive of *respect;* an Impression the most opposite to laughter that can be. This Impression then, it was, at all adventures, necessary to with-hold; which could not perhaps well be without dressing up these qualities in fantastic forms, and colours not their own; and thereby cheating the eye with shews of baseness and of folly, whilst he stole as it were upon the palate a richer and a fuller *goût*. To this end, what arts, what contrivances, has he not practised! How has he steeped this singular character in bad habits for fifty years together, and brought him forth saturated with every folly and with every vice not destructive of his essential character, or incompatible with his own primary design! For this end, he has deprived *Falstaff* of every good principle; and for another, which will be presently mentioned, he has concealed every bad one. He has given him also every infirmity of body that is not likely to awaken our compassion, and which is most proper to render both his better qualities and his vices ridiculous: He has associated levity and debauch with *age,* corpulence and inactivity with *courage,* and has roguishly coupled the gout with *Military honours,* and a *pension* with the *pox.* He has likewise involved this character in situations, out of which neither wit or Courage can extricate him with honour. The surprize at *Gads-hill* might have betrayed a hero into flight, and the encounter with *Douglas* left him no choice but death or stratagem. If he plays an after-game, and endeavours to redeem his ill fortune by lies and braggadocio, his ground fails him; no wit, no evasion will avail: Or is he likely to appear respectable in his person, rank, and demeanor, how is that respect abated or discharged! *Shakespeare* has given him a kind of state indeed; but of what is it composed: Of that fustian cowardly rascal *Pistol,* and his yoke-fellow of few words the equally deedless *Nym;* of his cup-bearer the fiery *Trigon,* whose zeal burns in his nose, *Bardolph;* and of the boy, who bears the purse with *seven groats and two-pence;*—a boy who was given him on purpose to set him off, and whom he walks *before,* according to his own description, *"like a sow that had overwhelmed all her litter but one."*

But it was not enough to render *Falstaff* ridiculous in his figure, situations, and equipage; *still* his respectable qualities would have come forth, at least occasionally, to spoil our mirth; or they might have burst the intervention of such slight impediments, and have every where shone through: It was necessary then to go farther, and throw on him that substantial ridicule, which only the incongruities of real vice can furnish; of vice, which was to be so mixed and blended with his frame as to give a durable character and colour to the whole.

But it may here be necessary to detain the reader a moment in order to apprize him of my further intention; without which, I might hazard that good understanding, which I hope has hitherto been preserved between us.

I have 'till now looked only to the Courage of *Falstaff,* a quality which having been denied, in terms, to belong to his constitution, I have endeavoured to vindicate to the Understandings of my readers; the Impression on their Feelings (in which all Dramatic truth consists) being already, as I have supposed, in favour of the character. In the pursuit of this subject I have taken the general Impression of the whole character pretty much, I suppose, like other men; and, when occasion has required, have so transmitted it to the reader; joining in the common Feeling of *Falstaff's* pleasantry, his apparent freedom from ill principle, and his companionable wit and good humour: With a stage character, in the article of exhibition, we have nothing more to do; for in fact what is it but an Impression; an appearance, which we are to consider as a reality; and which we may venture to applaud or condemn as such, without further inquiry or investigation? But if we would account for our Impressions, or for certain sentiments or actions in a character, not derived from its apparent principles, yet appearing, we know not why, natural, we are then compelled to look farther, and examine if there be not something more in the character than is *shewn;* something inferred, which is not brought under our special notice: In short, we must look to the art of the writer, and to the principles of human nature, to discover the hidden causes of such effects.—Now this is a very different matter— The former considerations respected the Impression only, without regard to the Understanding; but this question relates to the Understanding alone. It is true that there are but few Dramatic characters which will bear this kind of investigation, as not being drawn in exact conformity to those principles of general nature to which we must refer. But this is not the case with regard to the characters of *Shakespeare;* they are struck out *whole,* by some happy art which I cannot clearly comprehend, out of the general mass of things, from the block as it were of nature: And it is, I think, an easier thing to give a just draught of man from these Theatric forms, which I cannot help considering as originals, than by drawing from real life, amidst so much intricacy, obliquity, and disguise. If therefore, for further proofs of *Falstaff's* Courage, or for the sake of curious speculation, or for both, I change my position, and look to causes instead of effects, the reader must not be surprized if he finds the former *Falstaff* vanish like a dream, and another, of more disgustful form, presented to his view; one, whose final punishment we shall be so far from regretting, that we ourselves shall be ready to consign him to a severer doom.

The reader will very easily apprehend that a character, which we might wholly disapprove of, considered as existing in human life, may yet be thrown on the stage into certain peculiar situations, and be compressed by external influences into such temporary appearances, as may render such character for a time highly acceptable and entertaining, and even more distinguished for qualities, which on this supposition would be accidents only, than another character really possessing those qualities, but which, under the pressure of the same situation and influences, would be distorted into a different form, or totally lost in timidity and weakness. If therefore the character before us will admit of this kind of investigation, our Inquiry will not be without some dignity, considered as extending to the principles of human nature, and to the genius and arts of Him, who has best caught every various form of the human mind, and transmitted them with the greatest happiness and fidelity. . . .

Such, I think, is the true character of this extraordinary buffoon; and from hence we may discern for what special purposes *Shakespeare* has given him talents and qualities, which were to be afterwards obscured, and perverted to ends opposite to their nature; it was clearly to furnish out a Stage buffoon of a peculiar sort; a kind of Game-bull which would stand the baiting thro' a hundred Plays, and produce equal sport, whether he is pinned down occasionally by *Hal* or *Poins,* or tosses such mongrils as *Bardolph,* or the Justices, sprawling in the air. There is in truth no such thing as totally demolishing *Falstaff;* he has so much of the invulnerable in his frame that no ridicule can destroy him; he is safe even in defeat, and seems to rise, like another *Antæus,* with recruited vigour from every fall; in this as in every other respect, unlike *Parolles* or *Bobadil:* They fall by the first shaft of ridicule, but *Falstaff* is a butt on which we may empty the whole quiver, whilst the substance of his character remains unimpaired. His ill habits, and the accidents of age and corpulence, are no part of his essential constitution; they come forward indeed on our eye, and solicit our notice, but they are second natures, not *first;* mere shadows, we pursue them in vain; *Falstaff* himself has a distinct and separate subsistence; he laughs at the chace, and when the sport is over, gathers them with unruffled feather under his wing: And hence it is that he is made to undergo not one detection only, but a series of detections; that he is not formed for one Play only, but was intended originally at least for two; and the author we are told, was doubtful if he should not extend him yet farther, and engage him in the wars with *France.* This he might well have done, for there is nothing perishable in the nature of *Falstaff:* He might have involved him, by the vicious part of his character, in new difficulties and unlucky situations, and have enabled him, by the better part, to have scrambled through, abiding and retorting the jests and laughter of every beholder. . . .

But whatever be the question, or whatever the character, the curtain must not only be dropt before the eyes, but over the minds of the spectators, and nothing left for further examination and curiosity.—But how was this to be done in regard to *Falstaff?* He was not involved in the fortune of the Play; he was engaged in no action which, as to him, was to be compleated; he had reference to no system, he was attracted to no center; he passes thro' the Play as a lawless meteor, and we wish to know what course he is afterwards likely to take: He is detected and disgraced, it is true; but he lives by detection, and thrives on disgrace; and we are desirous to see him detected and disgraced again. The *Fleet* might be no bad scene of further amusement;—he carries *all* within him, *and what matter* where, *if he be still the same,* possessing the same force of mind, the same wit, and the same incongruity. This, *Shakespeare* was fully sensible of, and knew that this character could not be compleatly dismissed but by death.—"Our author, (says the Epilogue to the Second Part of Henry IV.) will continue the story with Sir *John* in it, and make you merry with fair *Catherine* of *France;* where, for any thing I know, *Falstaff* shall dye of a sweat, unless already he be killed with your hard opinions." If it had been prudent in *Shakespeare* to have killed *Falstaff* with *hard opinion,* he had the means in his hand to effect it;—but dye, it seems, he must, in one form or another, and a *sweat* would have been no unsuitable catastrophe. However we have reason to be satisfied as it is;—his death was worthy of his birth and of his life: *"He was born,"* he says, *"about three o'clock in the afternoon with a white head, and something a round belly."* But if he came into the world in the evening with these marks of age, he departs out of it in the morning in all the follies and vanities of youth;—*"He was shaked"* (we are told) *"of a burning quotidian tertian;—the young King had run bad humours on the knight;—his heart was fracted and corroborate; and a' parted just between twelve and one, even at the turning of the tide, yielding the crow a pudding, and passing directly into* Arthur's bosom, *if ever man went into the bosom of* Arthur."—So ended this singular buffoon; and with him ends an Essay, on which the reader is left to bestow what character he pleases: An Essay professing to treat of the Courage of *Falstaff,* but extending itself to his Whole character; to the arts and genius of his Poetic-Maker, SHAKESPEARE; and thro' him sometimes, with ambitious aim, even to the principles of human nature itself.

SAMUEL JOHNSON

The Rejection and Character of Falstaff

ACT V. SCENE viii. (v. v. 68.)
KING. *I banish thee, on pain of death.*

Mr. *Rowe* observes, that many readers lament to see *Falstaff* so hardly used by his old friend. But if it be considered that the fat knight has never uttered one sentiment of generosity, and with all his power of exciting mirth, has nothing in him that can be esteemed, no great pain will be suffered from the reflection that he is compelled to live honestly, and maintained by the king, with a promise of advancement when he shall deserve it.

I think the poet more blameable for *Poins,* who is always represented as joining some virtues with his vices, and is therefore treated by the prince with apparent distinction, yet he does nothing in the time of action, and though after the bustle is over he is again a favourite, at last vanishes without notice. *Shakespeare* certainly lost him by heedlessness, in the multiplicity of his characters, the variety of his action, and his eagerness to end the play.

ACT V. SCENE ix. (v. v. 97.)
CHIEF JUSTICE. *Go, carry Sir* John Falstaff *to the* Fleet.

I do not see why *Falstaff* is carried to the Fleet. We have never lost sight of him since his dismission from the king; he has committed no new fault, and therefore incurred no punishment; but the different agitations of fear, anger, and surprise in him and his company, made a good scene to the eye; and our authour, who wanted them no longer on the stage, was glad to find this method of sweeping them away.

I fancy every reader, when he ends this play, cries out with *Desdemona, O most lame and impotent conclusion!* As this play was not, to our knowledge, divided into acts by the authour, I could be content to conclude it with the death of *Henry* the fourth.

From *Johnson on Shakespeare,* ed. W. Raleigh (Oxford, 1908; reprinted 1931), pp. 123–125. Title supplied by the present editor.

In that Jerusalem shall Harry *dye.* These scenes which now make the fifth act of *Henry* the fourth, might then be the first of *Henry* the fifth; but the truth is, that they do unite very commodiously to either play. When these plays were represented, I believe they ended as they are now ended in the books; but *Shakespeare* seems to have designed that the whole series of action from the beginning of *Richard* the second, to the end of *Henry* the fifth, should be considered by the reader as one work, upon one plan, only broken into parts by the necessity of exhibition.

None of *Shakespeare's* plays are more read than the first and second parts of *Henry* the fourth. Perhaps no authour has ever in two plays afforded so much delight. The great events are interesting, for the fate of kingdoms depends upon them; the slighter occurrences are diverting, and, except one or two, sufficiently probable; the incidents are multiplied with wonderful fertility of invention, and the characters diversified with the utmost nicety of discernment, and the profoundest skill in the nature of man.

The prince, who is the hero both of the comick and tragick part, is a young man of great abilities and violent passions, whose sentiments are right, though his actions are wrong; whose virtues are obscured by negligence, and whose understanding is dissipated by levity. In his idle hours he is rather loose than wicked, and when the occasion forces out his latent qualities, he is great without effort, and brave without tumult. The trifler is roused into a hero, and the hero again reposes in the trifler. This character is great, original, and just.

Piercy is a rugged soldier, cholerick, and quarrelsome, and has only the soldier's virtues, generosity and courage.

But *Falstaff* unimitated, unimitable *Falstaff,* how shall I describe thee? Thou compound of sense and vice; of sense which may be admired but not esteemed, of vice which may be despised, but hardly detested. *Falstaff* is a character loaded with faults, and with those faults which naturally produce contempt. He is a thief, and a glutton, a coward, and a boaster, always ready to cheat the weak, and prey upon the poor; to terrify the timorous and insult the defenceless. At once obsequious and malignant, he satirises in their absence those whom he lives by flattering. He is familiar with the prince only as an agent of vice, but of this familiarity he is so proud as not only to be supercilious and haughty with common men, but to think his interest of importance to the duke of *Lancaster.* Yet the man thus corrupt, thus despicable, makes himself necessary to the prince that despises him, by the most pleasing of all qualities, perpetual gaiety, by an unfailing power of exciting laughter, which is the more freely indulged, as his wit is not of the splendid or ambitious kind, but consists in easy escapes and sallies of levity, which make sport but raise no envy. It must be observed that he is stained with no enormous or sanguinary crimes, so that his licentiousness is not so offensive but that it may be borne for his mirth.

The moral to be drawn from this representation is, that no man is more dangerous than he that with a will to corrupt, hath the power to please; and that neither wit nor honesty ought to think themselves safe with such a companion when they see *Henry* seduced by *Falstaff*.

A. C. BRADLEY

The Rejection of Falstaff

. . . Now why did Shakespeare end his drama with a scene which, though undoubtedly striking, leaves an impression so unpleasant? I will venture to put aside without discussion the idea that he meant us throughout the two plays to regard Falstaff with disgust or indignation, so that we naturally feel nothing but pleasure at his fall; for this idea implies that kind of inability to understand Shakespeare with which it is idle to argue. And there is another and a much more ingenious suggestion which must equally be rejected as impossible. According to it, Falstaff, having listened to the King's speech, did not seriously hope to be sent for by him in private; he fully realised the situation at once, and was only making game of Shallow; and in his immediate turn upon Shallow when the King goes out, "Master Shallow, I owe you a thousand pound," we are meant to see his humorous superiority to any rebuff, so that we end the play with the delightful feeling that, while Henry has done the right thing, Falstaff, in his outward overthrow, has still proved himself inwardly invincible. This suggestion comes from a critic who understands Falstaff, and in the suggestion itself shows that he understands him. But it provides no solution, because it wholly ignores, and could not account for, that which follows the short conversation with Shallow. Falstaff's dismissal to the Fleet, and his subsequent death, prove beyond doubt that his rejection was meant by Shakespeare to be taken as a catastrophe which not even his humour could enable him to surmount.

Moreover, these interpretations, even if otherwise admissible, would still leave our problem only partly solved. For what troubles us is not only the disappointment of Falstaff, it is the conduct of Henry. It was inevitable that on his accession he should separate himself from Sir John, and we wish nothing else. It is satisfactory that Sir John should have a competence, with the hope of promotion in the highly improbable case

From *Oxford Lectures on Poetry* (Macmillan & Company Ltd., 1909), pp. 252–273. Reprinted by permission of St. Martin's Press, Inc. Footnotes have been omitted. The essay has been somewhat abridged.

of his reforming himself. And if Henry could not trust himself within ten miles of so fascinating a companion, by all means let him be banished that distance: we do not complain. These arrangements would not have prevented a satisfactory ending: the King could have communicated his decision, and Falstaff could have accepted it, in a private interview rich in humour and merely touched with pathos. But Shakespeare has so contrived matters that Henry could not send a private warning to Falstaff even if he wished to, and in their public meeting Falstaff is made to behave in so infatuated and outrageous a manner that great sternness on the King's part was unavoidable. And the curious thing is that Shakespeare did not stop here. If this had been all we should have felt pain for Falstaff, but not, perhaps, resentment against Henry. But two things we do resent. Why, when this painful incident seems to be over, should the Chief Justice return and send Falstaff to prison? Can this possibly be meant for an act of private vengeance on the part of the Chief Justice, unknown to the King? No; for in that case Shakespeare would have shown at once that the King disapproved and cancelled it. It must have been the King's own act. This is one thing we resent; the other is the King's sermon. He had a right to turn away his former self, and his old companions with it, but he had no right to talk all of a sudden like a clergyman; and surely it was both ungenerous and insincere to speak of them as his "misleaders," as though in the days of Eastcheap and Gadshill he had been a weak and silly lad. We have seen his former self, and we know that it was nothing of the kind. He had shown himself, for all his follies, a very strong and independent young man, deliberately amusing himself among men over whom he had just as much ascendency as he chose to exert. Nay, he amused himself not only among them, but at their expense. In his first soliloquy—and first soliloquies are usually significant—he declares that he associates with them in order that, when at some future time he shows his true character, he may be the more wondered at for his previous aberrations. You may think he deceives himself here; you may believe that he frequented Sir John's company out of delight in it and not merely with this coldblooded design; but at any rate he *thought* the design was his one motive. And, that being so, two results follow. He ought in honour long ago to have given Sir John clearly to understand that they must say good-bye on the day of his accession. And, having neglected to do this, he ought not to have lectured him as his misleader. It was not only ungenerous, it was dishonest. It looks disagreeably like an attempt to buy the praise of the respectable at the cost of honour and truth. And it succeeded. Henry *always* succeeded.

You will see what I am suggesting, for the moment, as a solution of our problem. I am suggesting that our fault lies not in our resentment at Henry's conduct, but in our surprise at it; that if we had read his character truly in the light that Shakespeare gave us, we should have been prepared for a display both of hardness and of policy at this point in his career. And although this suggestion does not suffice to solve the problem before us, I am convinced that in itself it is true. Nor is it rendered at all improbable by the fact that Shakespeare has made Henry, on the whole, a fine and very attractive character, and that here he makes no one express any disapprobation of the treatment of Falstaff. For in similar cases Shakespeare is constantly misunderstood. His readers expect him to mark in some distinct way his approval or disapproval of that which he represents; and hence where *they* disapprove and *he* says nothing, they fancy that he does *not* disapprove, and they blame his indifference, like Dr. Johnson, or at the least are puzzled. But the truth is that he shows the fact and leaves the judgment to them. And again, when he makes us like a character we expect the character to have no faults that are not expressly pointed out, and when other faults appear we either ignore them or try to explain them away. This is one of our methods of conventionalising Shakespeare. We want the world's population to be neatly divided into sheep and goats, and we want an angel by us to say, "Look, that is a goat and this is a sheep," and we try to turn Shakespeare into this angel. His impartiality makes us uncomfortable: we cannot bear to see him, like the sun, lighting up everything and judging nothing. And this is perhaps especially the case in his historical plays, where we are always trying to turn him into a partisan. He shows us that Richard II. was unworthy to be king, and we at once conclude that he thought Bolingbroke's usurpation justified; whereas he shows merely, what under the conditions was bound to exist, an inextricable tangle of right and unright. Or, Bolingbroke being evidently wronged, we suppose Bolingbroke's statements to be true, and are quite surprised when, after attaining his end through them, he mentions casually on his death-bed that they were lies. Shakespeare makes us admire Hotspur heartily; and accordingly when we see Hotspur discussing with others how large his particular slice of his mother-country is to be, we either fail to recognise the monstrosity of the proceeding, or, recognizing it, we complain that Shakespeare is inconsistent. Prince John breaks a tottering rebellion by practising a detestable fraud on the rebels. We are against the rebels, and have heard high praise of Prince John, but we cannot help seeing that his fraud is detestable; so we say indignantly to Shakespeare, "Why, you told us he was a sheep"; whereas, in fact, if we had used our eyes we should have known beforehand that he was the brave, determined, loyal, cold-blooded, pitiless, unscrupulous son of a usurper whose throne was in danger.

To come, then, to Henry. Both as prince and as king he is deservedly a favourite, and particularly so with English readers, being, as he is, perhaps the most distinctively English of all Shakespeare's men. In *Henry*

V. he is treated as a national hero. In this play he has lost much of the wit which in him seems to have depended on contact with Falstaff, but he has also laid aside the most serious faults of his youth. He inspires in a high degree fear, enthusiasm, and affection; thanks to his beautiful modesty he has the charm which is lacking to another mighty warrior, Coriolanus; his youthful escapades have given him an understanding of simple folk, and sympathy with them; he is the author of the saying, "There is some soul of goodness in things evil"; and he is much more obviously religious than most of Shakespeare's heroes. Having these and other fine qualities, and being without certain dangerous tendencies which mark the tragic heroes, he is, perhaps, the most *efficient* character drawn by Shakespeare, unless Ulysses, in *Troilus and Cressida*, is his equal. And so he has been described as Shakespeare's ideal man of action; nay, it has even been declared that here for once Shakespeare plainly disclosed his own ethical creed, and showed us his ideal, not simply of a man of action, but of a man.

But Henry is neither of these. The poet who drew Hamlet and Othello can never have thought that even the ideal man of action would lack that light upon the brow which at once transfigures them and marks their doom. It is as easy to believe that, because the lunatic, the lover, and the poet are not far apart, Shakespeare would have chosen never to have loved and sung. Even poor Timon, the most inefficient of the tragic heroes, has something in him that Henry never shows. Nor is it merely that his nature is limited: if we follow Shakespeare and look closely at Henry, we shall discover with the many fine traits a few less pleasing. Henry IV. describes him as the noble image of his own youth; and, for all his superiority to his father, he is still his father's son, the son of the man whom Hotspur called a "vile politician." Henry's religion, for example, is genuine, it is rooted in his modesty; but it is also superstitious —an attempt to buy off supernatural vengeance for Richard's blood; and it is also in part political, like his father's projected crusade. Just as he went to war chiefly because, as his father told him, it was the way to keep factious nobles quiet and unite the nation, so when he adjures the Archbishop to satisfy him as to his right to the French throne, he knows very well that the Archbishop *wants* the war because it will defer and perhaps prevent what he considers the spoliation of the Church. This same strain of policy is what Shakespeare marks in the first soliloquy in *Henry IV.*, where the prince describes his riotous life as a mere scheme to win him glory later. It implies that readiness to use other people as means to his own ends which is a conspicuous feature in his father; and it reminds us of his father's plan of keeping himself out of the people's sight while Richard was making himself cheap by his incessant public appearances. And if I am not mistaken there is a further likeness. Henry is kindly and pleasant to every one as Prince, to every one

deserving as King; and he is so not merely out of policy: but there is
no sign in him of a strong affection for any one, such an affection as
we recognize at a glance in Hamlet and Horatio, Brutus and Cassius,
and many more. We do not find this in *Henry V.*, not even in the noble
address to Lord Scroop, and in *Henry IV.* we find, I think, a liking for
Falstaff and Poins, but no more: there is no more than a liking, for
instance, in his soliloquy over the supposed corpse of his fat friend, and
he never speaks of Falstaff to Poins with any affection. The truth is,
that the members of the family of Henry IV. have love for one another,
but they cannot spare love for any one outside their family, which stands
firmly united, defending its royal position against attack and instinctively
isolating itself from outside influence.

Thus I would suggest that Henry's conduct in his rejection of Falstaff
is in perfect keeping with his character on its unpleasant side as well as
on its finer; and that, so far as Henry is concerned, we ought not to feel
surprise at it. And on this view we may even explain the strange incident of the Chief Justice being sent back to order Falstaff to prison (for
there is no sign of any such uncertainty in the text as might suggest an
interpolation by the players). Remembering his father's words about
Henry, "Being incensed, he's flint," and remembering in *Henry V.* his
ruthlessness about killing the prisoners when he is incensed, we may
imagine that, after he had left Falstaff and was no longer influenced by
the face of his old companion, he gave way to anger at the indecent
familiarity which had provoked a compromising scene on the most ceremonial of occasions and in the presence alike of court and crowd, and
that he sent the Chief Justice back to take vengeance. And this is consistent with the fact that in the next play we find Falstaff shortly afterwards not only freed from prison, but unmolested in his old haunt in
Eastcheap, well within ten miles of Henry's person. His anger had soon
passed, and he knew that the requisite effect had been produced both
on Falstaff and on the world.

But all this, however true, will not solve our problem. It seems, on
the contrary, to increase its difficulty. For the natural conclusion is that
Shakespeare *intended* us to feel resentment against Henry. And yet that
cannot be, for it implies that he meant the play to end disagreeably;
and no one who understands Shakespeare at all will consider that supposition for a moment credible. No; he must have meant the play to
end pleasantly, although he made Henry's action consistent. And hence
it follows that he must have intended our sympathy with Falstaff to be
so far weakened when the rejection-scene arrives that his discomfiture
should be satisfactory to us; that we should enjoy this sudden reverse
of enormous hopes (a thing always ludicrous if sympathy is absent);
that we should approve the moral judgment that falls on him; and so
should pass lightly over that disclosure of unpleasant traits in the King's

character which Shakespeare was too true an artist to suppress. Thus
our pain and resentment, if we feel them, are wrong, in the sense that
they do not answer to the dramatist's intention. But it does not follow
that they are wrong in a further sense. They may be right, because the
dramatist has missed what he aimed at. And this, though the dramatist
was Shakespeare, is what I would suggest. In the Falstaff scenes he
overshot his mark. He created so extraordinary a being, and fixed him
so firmly on his intellectual throne, that when he sought to dethrone him
he could not. The moment comes when we are to look at Falstaff in a
serious light, and the comic hero is to figure as a baffled schemer; but
we cannot make the required change, either in our attitude or in our
sympathies. We wish Henry a glorious reign and much joy of his crew
of hypocritical politicians, lay and clerical; but our hearts go with Falstaff to the Fleet, or, if necessary, to Arthur's bosom or wheresomever
he is.

In the remainder of the lecture I will try to make this view clear.
And to that end we must go back to the Falstaff of the body of the two
plays, the immortal Falstaff, a character almost purely humorous, and
therefore no subject for moral judgments. I can but draw an outline,
and in describing one aspect of this character must be content to hold
another in reserve.

2.

Up to a certain point Falstaff is ludicrous in the same way as many
other figures, his distinction lying, so far, chiefly in the mere abundance
of ludicrous traits. *Why* we should laugh at a man with a huge belly
and corresponding appetites; at the inconveniences he suffers on a hot
day, or in playing the footpad, or when he falls down and there are no
levers at hand to lift him up again; at the incongruity of his unwieldy
bulk and the nimbleness of his spirit, the infirmities of his age and his
youthful lightness of heart; at the enormity of his lies and wiles, and
the suddenness of their exposure and frustration; at the contrast between his reputation and his real character, seen most absurdly when, at
the mere mention of his name, a redoubted rebel surrenders to him—
why, I say, we should laugh at these and many such things, this is no
place to inquire; but unquestionably we do. Here we have them poured
out in endless profusion and with that air of careless ease which is so
fascinating in Shakespeare; and with the enjoyment of them I believe
many readers stop. But while they are quite essential to the character,
there is in it much more. For these things by themselves do not explain
why, beside laughing at Falstaff, we are made happy by him and laugh
with him. He is not, like Parolles, a mere *object* of mirth.

The main reason why he makes us so happy and puts us so entirely
at our ease is that he himself is happy and entirely at his ease. "Happy"

is too weak a word; he is in bliss, and we share his glory. Enjoyment—
no fitful pleasure crossing a dull life, nor any vacant convulsive mirth—
but a rich deep-toned chuckling enjoyment circulates continually through
all his being. If you ask *what* he enjoys, no doubt the answer is, in the
first place, eating and drinking, taking his ease at his inn, and the company of other merry souls. Compared with these things, what we count
the graver interests of life are nothing to him. But then, while we are
under his spell, it is impossible to consider these graver interests; gravity
is to us, as to him, inferior to gravy; and what he does enjoy he enjoys
with such a luscious and good-humoured zest that we sympathise and
he makes us happy. And if any one objected, we should answer with
Sir Toby Belch, "Dost thou think, because thou art virtuous, there shall
be no more cakes and ale?"

But this, again, is far from all. Falstaff's ease and enjoyment are not
simply those of the happy man of appetite; they are those of the humorist, and the humorist of genius. Instead of being comic to you and serious to himself, he is more ludicrous to himself than to you; and he makes
himself out more ludicrous than he is, in order that he and others may
laugh. Prince Hal never made such sport of Falstaff's person as he himself did. It is *he* who says that his skin hangs about him like an old
lady's loose gown, and that he walks before his page like a sow that hath
o'erwhelmed all her litter but one. And he jests at himself when he is
alone just as much as when others are by. It is the same with his appetites. The direct enjoyment they bring him is scarcely so great as the
enjoyment of laughing at this enjoyment; and for all his addiction to sack
you never see him for an instant with a brain dulled by it, or a temper
turned solemn, silly, quarrelsome, or pious. The virtue it instils into him,
of filling his brain with nimble, fiery, and delectable shapes—this, and
his humorous attitude towards it, free him, in a manner, from slavery
to it; and it is this freedom, and no secret longing for better things
(those who attribute such a longing to him are far astray), that makes
his enjoyment contagious and prevents our sympathy with it from being
disturbed.

The bliss of freedom gained in humour is the essence of Falstaff. His
humour is not directed only or chiefly against obvious absurdities; he is
the enemy of everything that would interfere with his ease, and therefore of anything serious, and especially of everything respectable and
moral. For these things impose limits and obligations, and make us the
subjects of old father antic the law, and the categorical imperative, and
our station and its duties, and conscience, and reputation, and other
people's opinions, and all sorts of nuisances. I say he is therefore their
enemy; but I do him wrong; to say that he is their enemy implies that
he regards them as serious and recognises their power, when in truth he
refuses to recognize them at all. They are to him absurd; and to reduce
a thing *ad absurdum* is to reduce it to nothing and to walk about free

and rejoicing. This is what Falstaff does with all the would-be serious things of life, sometimes only by his words, sometimes by his actions too. He will make truth appear absurd by solemn statements, which he utters with perfect gravity and which he expects nobody to believe; and honour, by demonstrating that it cannot set a leg, and that neither the living nor the dead can possess it; and law, by evading all the attacks of its highest representative and almost forcing him to laugh at his own defeat; and patriotism, by filling his pockets with the bribes offered by competent soldiers who want to escape service, while he takes in their stead the halt and maimed and the gaol-birds; and duty, by showing how he labours in his vocation—of thieving; and courage, alike by mocking at his own capture of Colvile and gravely claiming to have killed Hotspur; and war, by offering the Prince his bottle of sack when he is asked for a sword; and religion, by amusing himself with remorse at odd times when he has nothing else to do; and the fear of death, by maintaining perfectly untouched, in the face of imminent peril and even while he *feels* the fear of death, the very same power of dissolving it in persiflage that he shows when he sits at ease in his inn. These are the wonderful achievements which he performs, not with the discontent of a cynic, but with the gaiety of a boy. And, therefore, we praise him, we laud him, for he offends none but the virtuous, and denies that life is real or life is earnest, and delivers us from the oppression of such nightmares, and lifts us into the atmosphere of perfect freedom.

No one in the play understands Falstaff fully, any more than Hamlet was understood by the persons round him. They are both men of genius. Mrs. Quickly and Bardolph are his slaves, but they know not why. "Well, fare thee well," says the hostess whom he has pillaged and forgiven; "I have known thee these twenty-nine years, come peas-cod time, but an honester and truer-hearted man—well, fare thee well." Poins and the Prince delight in him; they get him into corners for the pleasure of seeing him escape in ways they cannot imagine; but they often take him much too seriously. Poins, for instance, rarely sees, the Prince does not always see, and moralising critics never see, that when Falstaff speaks ill of a companion behind his back, or writes to the Prince that Poins spreads it abroad that the Prince is to marry his sister, he knows quite well that what he says will be repeated, or rather, perhaps, is absolutely indifferent whether it be repeated or not, being certain that it can only give him an opportunity for humour. It is the same with his lying, and almost the same with his cowardice, the two main vices laid to his charge even by sympathisers. Falstaff is neither a liar nor a coward in the usual sense, like the typical cowardly boaster of comedy. He tells his lies either for their own humour, or on purpose to get himself into a difficulty. He rarely expects to be believed, perhaps never. He abandons a statement or contradicts it the moment it is made. There is scarcely more intent in his lying than in the humorous exaggerations which he pours out in soliloquy just as much as when others are by. Poins and the Prince understand this in part. You see them waiting eagerly to convict him, not that they may really put him to shame, but in order to enjoy the greater lie that will swallow up the less. But their sense of humour lags behind his. Even the Prince seems to accept as half-serious that remorse of his which passes so suddenly into glee at the idea of taking a purse, and his request to his friend to bestride him if he should see him down in the battle. Bestride Falstaff! "Hence! Wilt thou lift up Olympus" . . . ?

3.

The main source, then, of our sympathetic delight in Falstaff is his humorous superiority to everything serious, and the freedom of soul enjoyed in it. But, of course, this is not the whole of his character. Shakespeare knew well enough that perfect freedom is not to be gained in this manner; we are ourselves aware of it even while we are sympathising with Falstaff; and as soon as we regard him seriously it becomes obvious. His freedom is limited in two main ways. For one thing he cannot rid himself entirely of respect for all that he professes to ridicule. He shows a certain pride in his rank: unlike the Prince, he is haughty to the drawers, who call him a proud Jack. He is not really quite indifferent to reputation. When the Chief Justice bids him pay his debt to Mrs. Quickly for his reputation's sake, I think he feels a twinge, though to be sure he proceeds to pay her by borrowing from her. He is also stung by any thoroughly serious imputation on his courage, and winces at the recollection of his running away on Gadshill; he knows that his behaviour there certainly looked cowardly, and perhaps he remembers that he would not have behaved so once. It is, further, very significant that, for all his dissolute talk, he has never yet allowed the Prince and Poins to *see* him as they saw him afterwards with Doll Tearsheet; not, of course, that he has any moral shame in the matter, but he knows that in such a situation he, in his old age, must appear contemptible—not a humorist but a mere object of mirth. And, finally, he has affection in him—affection, I think, for Poins and Bardolph, and certainly for the Prince; and that is a thing which he cannot jest out of existence. Hence, as the effect of his rejection shows, he is not really invulnerable. And then, in the second place, since he is in the flesh, his godlike freedom has consequences and conditions; consequences, for there is something painfully wrong with his great toe; conditions, for he cannot eat and drink for ever without money, and his purse suffers from consumption, a disease for which he can find no remedy. As the Chief Justice tells him, his means are very slender and his waste great; and his answer, "I would it were otherwise; I would my means were greater and my waist slenderer," though worth much money, brings none in. And so he is driven to evil deeds; not only to cheating his tailor like a gentleman, but to fleecing Justice Shallow, and to highway robbery, and to cruel depredations on the poor woman whose affection he has secured. All this is perfectly consistent with the other side of his character, but by itself it makes an ugly picture.

Yes, it makes an ugly picture when you look at it seriously. But then, surely, so long as the humorous atmosphere is preserved and the humorous attitude maintained, you do not look at it so. You no more regard Falstaff's misdeeds morally than you do the much more atrocious misdeeds of Punch or Reynard the Fox. You do not exactly ignore them, but you attend only to their comic aspect. This is the very spirit of comedy, and certainly of Shakespeare's comic world, which is one of make-believe, not merely as his tragic world is, but in a further sense— a world in which gross improbabilities are accepted with a smile, and many things are welcomed as merely laughable which, regarded gravely, would excite anger and disgust. The intervention of a serious spirit breaks up such a world, and would destroy our pleasure in Falstaff's company. Accordingly through the greater part of these dramas Shakespeare carefully confines this spirit to the scenes of war and policy, and dismisses it entirely in the humorous parts. Hence, if *Henry IV.* had been a comedy like *Twelfth Night,* I am sure that he would no more have ended it with the painful disgrace of Falstaff than he ended *Twelfth Night* by disgracing Sir Toby Belch.

But *Henry IV.* was to be in the main a historical play, and its chief hero Prince Henry. In the course of it his greater and finer qualities were to be gradually revealed, and it was to end with beautiful scenes of reconciliation and affection between his father and him, and a final emergence of the wild Prince as a just, wise, stern, and glorious King. Hence, no doubt, it seemed to Shakespeare that Falstaff at last must be disgraced, and must therefore appear no longer as the invincible humorist, but as an object of ridicule and even of aversion. And probably also his poet's insight showed him that Henry, as he conceived him, *would* behave harshly to Falstaff in order to impress the world, especially when his mind had been wrought to a high pitch by the scene with his dying father and the impression of his own solemn consecration to great duties.

This conception was a natural and a fine one; and if the execution was not an entire success, it is yet full of interest. Shakespeare's purpose being to work a gradual change in our feelings towards Falstaff, and to tinge the humorous atmosphere more and more deeply with seriousness, we see him carrying out this purpose in the Second Part of *Henry IV.* Here he separates the Prince from Falstaff as much as he can, thus withdrawing him from Falstaff's influence, and weakening in our minds the connection between the two. In the First Part we constantly see them together; in the Second (it is a remarkable fact) only once before the rejection. Further, in the scenes where Henry appears apart from Falstaff, we watch him growing more and more grave, and awakening more and more poetic interest; while Falstaff, though his humour scarcely flags to the end, exhibits more and more of his seamy side. This is nowhere turned to the full light in Part I.; but in Part II. we see him as the heartless destroyer of Mrs. Quickly, as a ruffian seriously defying the Chief Justice because his position as an officer on service gives him power to do wrong, as the pike preparing to snap up the poor old dace Shallow, and (this is the one scene where Henry and he meet) as the worn-out lecher, not laughing at his servitude to the flesh but sunk in it. Finally, immediately before the rejection, the world where he is king is exposed in all its sordid criminality when we find Mrs. Quickly and Doll arrested for being concerned in the death of one man, if not more, beaten to death by their bullies; and the dangerousness of Falstaff is emphasised in his last words as he hurries from Shallow's house to London, words at first touched with humour but at bottom only too seriously meant: "Let us take any man's horses; the laws of England are at my commandment. Happy are they which have been my friends, and woe unto my Lord Chief Justice." His dismissal to the Fleet by the Chief Justice is the dramatic vengeance for that threat.

Yet all these excellent devices fail. They cause us momentary embarrassment at times when repellent traits in Falstaff's character are disclosed; but they fail to change our attitude of humour into one of seriousness, and our sympathy into repulsion. And they were bound to fail, because Shakespeare shrank from adding to them the one device which would have ensured success. If, as the Second Part of *Henry IV.* advanced, he had clouded over Falstaff's humour so heavily that the man of genius turned into the Falstaff of the *Merry Wives*, we should have witnessed his rejection without a pang. This Shakespeare was too much of an artist to do—though even in this way he did something— and without this device he could not succeed. As I said, in the creation of Falstaff he overreached himself. He was caught up on the wind of his own genius, and carried so far that he could not descend to earth at the intended spot. It is not a misfortune that happens to many authors, nor is it one we can regret, for it costs us but a trifling inconvenience in one scene, while we owe to it perhaps the greatest comic character in literature. For it is in this character, and not in the judgment he brings upon Falstaff's head, that Shakespeare asserts his supremacy. To show that Falstaff's freedom of soul was in part illusory, and that the realities of life refused to be conjured away by his humour—this was what we might expect from Shakespeare's unfailing sanity, but it was surely no achievement beyond the power of lesser men. The achievement was Falstaff himself, and the conception of that freedom of soul, a freedom illusory only in part, and attainable only by a mind which had received from Shakespeare's own the inexplicable touch of infinity which he bestowed on Hamlet and Macbeth and Cleopatra, but denied to Henry the Fifth.

J. I. M. STEWART

The Birth and Death of Falstaff

> *So well hath Shakespeare expressed all sorts of persons as
> one would think he had been transformed into every one of
> those he hath described. . . . Who would not think he had
> been such a man as Sir John Falstaff?*
>
> MARGARET, DUCHESS OF NEWCASTLE (1624?–1674)

In DRAMATISING the material of *1 & 2 Henry IV* and *Henry V* Shakespeare did not start entirely from scratch. We know almost nothing except this bare fact. *The Famous Victories,* or something very like it, may
have been his "source," but it is possible that he worked from an earlier
and fuller play of which *The Famous Victories* is a vestigial version.[1]
When he created Sir John Falstaff, therefore, it is impossible to say
whether he had before him anything more full-bodied than the shadowy
comic material in the old play preserved to us. Nor can we tell whether
he returned to his own text and revised it in the light of his maturing
comic genius. Thus of what may be termed the gestation of Falstaff,
and of his delivery whether lenitive or hard, only conjecture speaks.
If his mother, when she looked down one three of the clock in the afternoon upon that white head and something round belly, murmured

> Where do you come from, baby dear?—

she was only anticipating the question of many learned men on what
dark night of forebeing first formed Sir John. Where does Falstaff come
from? This is the grand problem of Falstaff's *birth* which Maurice Morgann really raised in the eighteenth century when he wrote an essay (he

---

From *Character and Motive in Shakespeare* (London, 1949), pp. 111–144. Reprinted by
permission of Longmans, Green, and Company. Two footnotes have been omitted.

[1] The resemblances between *The Famous Victories* and Shakespeare's trilogy are detailed
by B. M. Ward in *Review of English Studies* (1928), iv, 270–94. On the question of
Shakespeare's possible revision of his own work see A. E. Morgan, *Some Problems of
Shakespeare's "Henry IV"* (Shakespeare Association Pamphlet, 1924).

says) "professing to treat of the Courage of *Falstaff*, but extending itself to his Whole character." There is another problem, that of Falstaff's *death*, which the nineteenth century first became aware of. Some examination of critical approaches to these two problems will occupy this final chapter.

1

And first there is the view—to be mentioned only briefly—that Falstaff had his birth in what is nowadays called a "documentary"; that he is the offspring of a devoted social historian. This is maintained by Mr. John W. Draper, who holds that Shakespeare "aimed merely to depict men and things as they are," and then draws the hazardous inference that it was therefore his sufficient business to depict them as they stood sorted and categorised in the Elizabethan social consciousness.[2] Here, I think, is a modified form of the old doctrine of *decorum* in imaginative literature. Shakespeare's characters, it seems, must stand or fall according as they do or do not correctly embody the various traits proper to certain sorts of Elizabethan person. Research will show that they do this better than might casually be supposed. Research therefore enjoys the pleasant consciousness of backing Shakespeare up. And as Falstaff is "an essentially realistic creation," and clearly intended to appear as an army officer,

> logically then, one should study his character as an army officer, rather than in any other group of Elizabethan society. . . . Army life was on a very low plane.

When one has made this study one will *expect* Falstaff to frequent disreputable people and places, pawn his military equipment, lead his men to slaughter in order to steal their "dead pay"—and so forth. One may also learn something of the probable attitude of the audience to the various aspects of Falstaff's depravity. Some of his later activities (those which critics have seen as more heinous and designed increasingly to stress the shadier side of the character) the audience would be disposed to condone. But his early behaviour at Gadshill they would wholly condemn—for does not Digges in his *Paradoxes* declare that "cowardize in Man (especially professing Armes) hath ever been accounted the foulest vice"? Here, then, is a pointer to how the audience regarded Sir John: "recognising him as a common type in the London of the day, they surely could not quite suspend the feelings and judgments that they associated with the living examples."

But this sort of criticism, I fear, takes us nowhere on the road we would go. If we are really concerned a little to account for Falstaff, if

2 John W. Draper, *Review of English Studies,* viii (1932), 414–24.

we would descry some shadow of answer to the question "Where does he come from?" we shall certainly find little help in Mr. Draper's approach, since the quality of what Shakespeare offers (and it is this alone that tempts us to any inquiry at all) is left out of account. Explanations must be something adequate to what is explained. But a patent inadequacy, as here, may put us on guard in more colourable places.

There is another view of Falstaff's engendering—a very compendious one—which may be mentioned before coming to substantial matters. Nothing was involved in the event except what gynaecologists call (I have been told) a pseudocyesis; nothing so indelicate as Falstaff's birth ever really occurred. Here we have the belief of the New Bowdlers, whom man delights not, no, nor woman neither, and who would give us not merely *Hamlet* without the Prince but the Complete Works without their several *dramatis personae*. "Falstaff," says Mr. L. C. Knights, "is not a man, but a choric commentary."[3] Conceivably he is both. But before a statement so exclusive we must take ground with the common reader, who knows that Falstaff is a substantial citizen of a world thronged with men and women—men and women, doubtless, who are not as we are; but the nature of whose reality would tax metaphysical disquisition. It has taxed the scholastic mind of Professor Stoll.

2

Stoll approaches Falstaff as a genealogist and a determinist, convinced that the man's path was laid down at his nativity. "Capitano Spavento," Stoll says to those curious about the knight's ancestry, "Spezzafer, Fracasso, Matamoros, Spezza-Monti, Giangurgolo, Vappo, Rogantino."[4] It sounds magnificent enough—a lineage which, armorially translated, should make a fine showing on that seal-ring of his grandfather's which Sir John always carried. Alas! these sounding names belong, it seems, to a line more ancient than honourable, one prominent in men's eyes since clowns first grinned through horse-collars or tumbled on a plank. Falstaff descends from the poltroons of literature, from the rascally bragging soldiers of Roman comedy, and he is bound hand and foot by his heredity. We know his ancestors and therefore we can predict his *Lebenstil*—his life-style, since this is determined by these. He cannot be other than cowardly, much as a Hapsburg cannot have other than such a lip and such a chin. For always the nurture which the individual artist brings to his creations is of small account compared with the nature which they derive from literary convention. In framing Falstaff Shakespeare preserves "immemorial custom," "the established *lazzi* of the coward on the stage . . . not in England only but in contemporary

3 [L. C. Knights, *How Many Children Had Lady Macbeth?* (1933), p. 21.]
4 E. E. Stoll, *Shakespeare Studies* (1927), chap. viii.

Germany, Spain, and Italy," "the traditional comic situation," "all the
conventional and traditional tricks of cowardice." Shakespeare had
neither impulse nor need to do otherwise, since this submitting to convention strengthens the artist and enables him to concentrate upon that
refinement within it which is his proper business:

> In the same period a great popular artist and a mediocre one use much
> the same means of expression—"business," situations and types. That is to
> say, the difference is in the touch.

And it is not in a psychological touch:

> Falstaff boasting and lying is treated typically, externally, . . . that he
> who chatters and scuffles in the pit may laugh and not fail.

Shakespeare was too conservative for *psychological* refinement—and this
makes cobweb of most modern criticism of Falstaff.

> In real life both Sir Johns [Oldcastle and Fastolf] were brave and worthy
> fellows; they are thus overwhelmed with obloquy because in the popular
> imagination one charge, as this of heresy or that of cowardice, brings every
> other in its trail; but all that concerns us here is that in Shakespeare they are
> cowards because they were that before. Always our poet stands by public
> opinion, and his English kings or Roman heroes are to him what they were
> to his age.

But do we, perhaps, find in Shakespeare what we seek? Stoll's quest
—his nose, we might say—is for "a convention, a bit of stage language
. . . precise and ascertainable." His Shakespeare accordingly is above
all things skilled in and subdued to "the stage language of his time—all
the traditions and associations of ideas"; Shakespeare is little more than
midwife to a fresh brood of these. The learning of Mr. Stoll has enabled
him to comprehend vividly the great theme of the continuity of literature, and his satisfaction in discerning the ordering finger of the centuries pointing Shakespeare his way has at times a quality almost enthusiastic and mystical. Why did Shakespeare write *The Merry Wives of
Windsor?* Because, the legend has it, the Queen called for a play of Sir
John Falstaff in love and Shakespeare, taking the luckless command in
the only possible way, dashed off a capital farce in a fortnight. For Stoll,
however, the old legend will not do.

> The figure of the braggart captain, which came into Shakespeare's hands
> from Plautus or from the Comedy of Masks, would have been incomplete if
> he had not appeared as the suitor gulled.

Is Falstaff, then, thus cramped in the buck-basket of a severe literary
determinism, simply a braggart captain paper-thin, and nothing more?
Stoll is far from saying this. "Falstaff . . . is not an ordinary stage

coward," he declares. Then in what does his distinction lie? Wherein *does* consist that "difference . . . in the touch"?

It is not, it seems, that Falstaff rises to any imperishable high comedy. Humour like his, picaresque humour, "morals and sentiments alike, in the lapse of time, obliterate." Either we must submit to a historical discipline and endeavour to arrive at Elizabethan notions of what is funny or we must submit to a "process of critical emasculation"—joining those who, "because of the tradition that he [Falstaff] is the supreme comic figure . . . have endeavoured and laboured to like him," or rather to like a sentimentalised substitute with a humorous constitution consonant with the manners of our time. Nevertheless Stoll must face the fact that Falstaff is a person of status in English dramatic history; that wherever cultivated people speak of Don Quixote and Panurge they are likely to speak of Falstaff too; that the knight is, in very fact, "Sir *Iohn* with all Europe." How is this to be accounted for?

It is the language, Stoll says; and it is here that we shall find an element really original to Shakespeare. What in Falstaff's appeal is immediate and perpetual

> lies not so much in his conduct as in his speech. He talks prose but is supremely poetic, and his is in many ways the most marvellous prose ever penned. It pulses with his vast vitality and irrepressible spirit, it glows with the warmth of his friendliness and good humour.

Now, this will hardly do. Falstaff, we have been told, is a stage coward, "treated typically, externally"; he is this redeemed by speech conceived as a magnificent garment concealing the stereotype within. But now (and in much more that Stoll finally says of "the magnetism of a personality," "the very spirit of comradeship," "the genius of converse") we are offered this great voice, this golden language as *expressing* personal qualities which the character may not, according to the hypothesis, *possess*. And here, it seems to me, is the central weakness of all Professor Stoll's criticism: it altogether misapprehends the creative situation; what is happening in the poet's mind when great voices begin to speak. Of course the poet uses language with a vast conscious craft to illustrate and adorn his conception. But just as, in poetry, the subtlety of the rhythm *is* the clarity of the emotion so, in drama, the voice *is* the character. We cannot penetrate through some rhetorical artifice in Falstaff to a spindle-shanked Capitano Spavento within, or catch him off guard, his wonderful speech hung

> loose about him, like a Giants Robe
> Upon a dwarfish Theefe.

Falstaff is something more than a dummy superlatively clothed, and Professor Stoll's theory of his birth is inadequate just as Mr. Draper's theory is inadequate, if less patently so. In Stoll's paper we are nowhere with Falstaff and nowhere with Shakespeare; we are with a Shakespeare from whom a specific creative power has been withdrawn. It is otherwise with Maurice Morgann's famous essay. This essay brings us close to Shakespeare. Or so I feel. And what I want to do now is to account to myself for this feeling. What makes this government official's whimsical defence of Falstaff's valour one of the great places in the criticism of Shakespeare?

Morgann, like Sir Max Beerbohm's Matthew Arnold, was not always wholly serious. He tells us that he "has endeavoured to preserve to his Text a certain lightness of air, and cheerfulness of tone," and moreover confesses himself "unengaged"—meaning thereby that he was among those "idle and unemployed" who were the most likely, according to the contemporary aesthetic, to take a fanciful view of things. Morgann's view of Falstaff is in aspects undeniably fanciful; it could hardly be otherwise since he sets out frankly in quest of literary diversion and defends his chosen paradox of Falstaff's constitutional courage with arguments which sometimes have only ingenuity and charm to recommend them. The vein of *bagatelle* which runs through the *Essay on the Dramatic Character of Sir John Falstaff* may prevent our acknowledging its essence: an understanding of where great dramatic creations have their birth.[5]

3

Morgann's foible is notorious: in his imagination he sees Falstaff as something very close to a historical personage. He discusses his off-stage activities, the fugitive and unexpressed impulses of his mind, the influences to which he would be exposed in boyhood as page to Thomas Mowbray, his lineage as it may be conjectured from scattered hints in the drama—inferring the *a priori* likelihood of his courage from "the circumstances and condition of his whole life and character. . . ."

> There is a certain roundness and integrity in the forms of *Shakespeare,* which give them an independence as well as a relation, insomuch that we often meet with passages which, tho' perfectly felt, cannot be sufficiently explained in words, without unfolding the whole character of the speaker. . . . The reader will not now be surprised if I affirm that those characters in *Shakespeare,* which are seen only in part, are yet capable of being unfolded and understood in the whole; every part being in fact relative, and inferring all the rest.

In other words it is permissible to consider Shakespeare's characters rather as Historic than Dramatic beings; and, when occasion requires, to

---

[5] Morgann's essay is reprinted in *Eighteenth Century Essays on Shakespeare,* ed. D. Nichol Smith (1903). Matthew Arnold appeared not always wholly serious to his niece, Miss Mary Augusta. . . .

account for their conduct from the *whole* of character, from general principles, from latent motives, and from policies not avowed.

In Shakespeare's characters, then, we are aware, just as we are in actual people, of depths and facets not immediately rendered in behaviour. They seem to carry about with them a fuller and more complex humanity than is required by the exigencies of their rôle. It is this that makes them so lifelike, and our intuitive apprehension of the *whole* character is an important part of our experience of the play. . . . A play —it may be declared by way of dismissing Morgann—is an artifice, not a document or historical record. And to suggest that we may work towards an actual whole by inference from the parts which alone have ever existed is merely whimsical. For the characters in a play, Shakespeare's as another's, have no being except as they, or the illusions of them, are conjured up before us by print on a page or by actors mouthing before a scene.

But is this manner of having done with Maurice Morgann and his haunting sense of some fuller being behind the outline on the stage (for that is the essence of his feeling) justifiable. . . ? Are the ways of the imagination indeed such that dramatic characters can partake of some larger life—a life of which only "secret impressions" are yielded in the theatre?

I think there is a sense in which we can, in fact, say of Shakespeare's great characters that "the parts which are not seen do . . . exist." An intuitive understanding of the processes of dramatic creation lies beneath the "lightness of air" of Morgann's *Essay* and makes it memorable as Shakespeare criticism.

4

Why does a man write plays or novels, after all; and how does he possess himself of the people who feel and act in them? On this Morgann himself has something to say—not much, but sufficient to set us on our road:

> But it was not enough for *Shakespeare* to have formed his characters with the most perfect truth and coherence; it was further necessary that he should possess a wonderful facility of compressing, as it were, his own spirit into these images, and of giving alternate animation to the forms. This was not to be done *from without;* he must have *felt* every varied situation, and have spoken thro' the organ he had formed. Such an intuitive comprehension of things and such a facility must unite to produce a *Shakespeare.* . . . The characters of *Shakespeare* are thus *whole,* and as it were original.

"Compressing, as it were, his own spirit into these images." Coleridge, Morgann's immediate successor in the great line of Shakespeare critics—

and another who believed that "Shakespeare's characters are like those in life, to be *inferred* by the reader"—takes us further when he notes

> Shakespeare's mode of conceiving characters out of his own intellectual and moral faculties, by conceiving any one intellectual or moral faculty in morbid excess and then placing himself, thus mutilated and diseased, under given circumstances.[6]

Coleridge's words here take colouring from their being directed at an elucidation of the character of Hamlet, but the perception underlying them is clear. The artist does not get the essence of his characters from camera-work, as Mr. Draper would suppose; nor yet from a filing-cabinet of traditional literary types, which is the belief Professor Stoll constantly expresses with what softening word he can. He gets his characters from an interplay of these with something inside. And it is because he has a particular sort of inside, or psychic constitution, that he is obliged to get them. Falstaff and his peers are the product of an imagination working urgently from within. The sum of the characters is a sort of sum—nay, gives something like the portrait—of Shakespeare: a truth which Walter Bagehot realises in his essay, *Shakespeare—the Man*.[7] ("If anybody could have any doubt about the liveliness of Shakespeare, let him consider the character of Falstaff.") But we do not quite express the matter by saying (what is obvious enough) that Shakespeare had immense perceptive and apperceptive power; that he could recognise in himself all the elements variously combined in the motley humanity about him, and so draw, with an original authority, the characters of many men and many women. To this we must add that there is typically in the artist an instability; a reluctance of elements, in themselves abnormally numerous, available and potent, to combine hierarchically in the formation of one permanent character; a corresponding impulse to build up now one and now another impermanent configuration of traits. "Now Master up, now Miss"—said Pope, projecting an extreme of this constitution upon his enemy. And here too is what Keats recognised as the chameleon nature of the poet.[8]

The inquiries of James and others into the phenomena of conversion, and of later investigators in the field of multiple and split personality (did Falstaff indeed have a Dr. Jekyll who drove the common tenement of clay hoarse with halloing and singing of anthems?) have shown how, in abnormal individuals not artistically endowed, either a co-presence or a succession of perfectly "real" personalities can be a psychological fact. And a man writes plays or novels, I conceive, partly at least because he is beset by unexpressed selves; by the subliminal falling now into one coherent pattern and now into another of the varied elements of his total

---

6 *Coleridge's Shakespearean Criticism*, ed. T. M. Raysor (1930), I, 37, 227.
7 *The Works and Life of Walter Bagehot* (1915), i, 239.
8 J. Keats, *Letters*, ed. M. Buxton Forman (1935), p. 228.

man—elements many of which will never, except in his writing, find play in consciousness.[9] It is this that gives the characters their "independence as well as relation"; their haunting suggestion of reality and of a larger, latent being unexhausted in the action immediately before us; their ability to beckon beyond the narrow limits of their hour. And here, too, we see how characters "come alive"—how Falstaff came alive. It was not that Shakespeare took a traditional figure and clothed it with the spurious animation of a dazzling dress. It was that he took that figure and infused into it as much—and only as much—of the Falstaff-being in himself as the exigencies of his design would admit. Of what more there was unused the bouquet, it may be, floats across the stage in those "secret impressions" which Morgann felt. And sherris and ambrosia mingle there.

We have discovered, I think, why Morgann's essay is so much nearer to Shakespeare than Stoll's. Morgann better understands being creative. Stoll sees Shakespeare making his book as Stoll would make a book: knowing just what he would do, assembling his material from all available sources, and then constructing according to the best professional specifications of his age. But Morgann knows that nothing was ever born alive this way, and that despite all the artist owes to tradition and convention his is an inner travail still. That he draws from tradition is assured, and he will be the better, perhaps, for having before him the idea of the literary kind to which he would contribute. But *what* he contributes will be his own, or nothing in art. It will be radically his own, and not an old thing resurfaced. For the essence of his task is in exploring an inward abundance. When he does this in drama his characters, sympathetically received, will inevitably suggest to us a life beyond the limits of their rôle. And Shakespeare, from the vast heaven of his mind, expresses whole constellations of emotion in personative form; it is nothing other than this that Morgann means when he asks:

For what is *Falstaff*, what *Lear,* what *Hamlet,* or *Othello,* but different modifications of *Shakespeare's* thought?

5

Before the death of Falstaff comes what is commonly regarded as its

[9] Freud notes of imaginative writers their tendency "to split up their ego by self-observation into many component-egos, and in this way to personify the conflicting trends in their own mental life in many heroes." [*Collected Papers* (1924), iv, 180.] The work of art—and typically a tragedy—is thus analytical, and the clarification it effects allows of something the same sort of beneficial emotional discharge as should occur in the course of analytic therapy. But it may be that in taking this view Freud, like Bridges after another fashion, is unconsciously subjecting himself to "the longest tyranny that ever swayed" and considering too exclusively Aristotle's theory of catharsis. We must not neglect the probability that tragedy evinces also the simpler mechanism of the ordeal. Thomas Hardy's belief that "If way to the Better there be, it exacts a full look at the Worst" is certainly operative when we sit through *King Lear* or *Othello.*

precipitating cause, his rejection—which we shall find, however, not so much the cause of death as a death itself. . . . It is much more uncomfortable than the corresponding speech in the "old play" preserved to us as *The Famous Victories:*

> *Hen. 5.* I prethee Ned, mend thy maners,
> And be more modester in thy tearmes,
> For my vnfeined greefe is not to be ruled by thy flattering
> And dissembling talke, thou saist I am changed,
> So I am indeed, and so must thou be, and that quickly,
> Or else I must cause thee to be chaunged.
> *Ioc.* Gogs wounds how like yo this?
> Sownds tis not so sweete as Musicke.
> *Tom.* I trust we haue not offended your grace no way.
> *Hen. 5.* Ah *Tom,* your former life greeues me,
> And makes me to abandon & abolish your company for euer
> By ten miles space, then if I heare wel of you,
> It may be I wil do somewhat for you,
> Otherwise looke for no more fauour at my hands,
> Then at any other mans: And therefore be gone,
> We haue other matters to talke on.

Tolstoy found the old *King Leir* at least less bad than Shakespeare's play;[10] and here, in the deal of skimble-skamble stuff that makes up *The Famous Victories,* is something more decent and subdued than Shakespeare's version. But it is something, of course, immensely less effective. The first thing to note is that, in his rejection, Shakespeare pulls out all the stops of his instrument. It is a resounding *coda,* the discovery and anatomy of which as a *problem* makes one of the curious chapters in modern Shakespeare criticism.

6

Were we to pursue this problem about our university cities to-day we should encounter a remarkable succession of conflicting voices, and this particularly in the crucial matter of Prince Henry's character and motive. At Oxford, or in its environs, we might meet the Poet Laureate, who has declared that

> Prince Henry is not a hero, he is not a thinker, he is not even a friend; he is a common man whose incapacity for feeling enables him to change his habits whenever interest bids him. Throughout the first acts he is careless and callous, though he is breaking his father's heart and endangering his father's throne. . . . He impresses one as quite common, quite selfish, quite without feeling. When he learns that his behaviour may have lost him his prospective crown, he passes a sponge over his past and fights like a wildcat for the right of not having to work for a living.[11]

10 [Tolstoy's *Shakespeare and the Drama* is reprinted by A. Maude in *Tolstoy on Art* [1924].]
11 J. Masefield, *Shakespeare* (1912), pp. 112–13.

Were we to move to Edinburgh we might hear Professor Dover Wilson, incomparable Sherlock Holmes among Shakespeare's editors, liken this same young prince to Spenser's Red Cross Knight, declare his regeneration to be "reasonable and human," his character "the soul of true honour," the manner of Falstaff's rejection "a happy solution," his committal to the Fleet "even something of a compliment," and any opinions maintained to the contrary to-day to be "characteristically muddle-headed."[12] Were we next to travel south to Manchester we might be admitted to the lecture-room of Professor Charlton, who finds in the rejection not a happy solution but the issue of "cumulative priggishness" and "callous cruelty" after which it is "unthinkable that our feelings towards [Prince Hal] can remain sympathetically genial." "It seems a safe guess that such a Hal, so false to Falstaff, will of that seed grow to a greater falseness. If indeed, a greater falseness is within the scope of conjecture."[13]

So much for the soul of true honour and for the Red Cross Knight. In London we could, unhappily, no longer hear a voice which some fifteen years ago told us that Hal is "the kind of personality that can no more be smircht by circumstance than white-hot iron by dust"; nor in Cambridge one which on the contrary roundly declared Hal's rejection of Falstaff to be suspiciously synchronous with Shakespeare's preparing to leave London, buying property in Stratford and generally turning respectable.[14] And Quiller-Couch pointed, as many critics have done, to a root of our discomforts in Hal's soliloquy at the close of *1 Henry IV*, Act I, ii. "I know you all," Hal says, when Falstaff, Poins and the rest have gone out—

> I know you all, and wil a while vphold
> The vnyokt humour of your idlenes,
> Yet herein wil I imitate the sunne,
> Who doth permit the base contagious clouds
> To smother vp his beauties from the world,
> That when he please againe to be himselfe,
> Being wanted he may be more wondred at . . .

"The most damnable piece of workmanship to be found in any of his plays," Quiller-Couch declares of this speech, and continues:

This, if we accept it, poisons what follows, poisons the madcap Prince in our imagination for good and all. Most of us can forgive youth, hot blood, riot: but a prig of a rake, rioting on a calculated scale, confessing that he does it coldly, intellectually, and that he proposes to desert his comrades at

[12] J. Dover Wilson, *The Fortunes of Falstaff* (1943).
[13] H. B. Charlton, *Shakespearian Comedy* (1938), chap. vii.
[14] The references are to Lascelles Abercrombie ["A Plea for the Liberty of Interpreting," *Proceedings of the British Academy* (1930), p. 137.] and Sir Arthur Quiller-Couch, *Shakespeare's Workmanship* (1918), chap. vii.

the right moment to better his own repute—*that* kind of rake surely all honest men abhor. . . .

We cannot keep them [the lines of the soliloquy] and keep any opinion of Henry as a decent fellow. . . . Falstaff had never consciously hurt Henry, had never—so far from unkindness—thought of him but kindly. Wisely or not—wisely, if we will—Henry had hurt Falstaff to death: and not for any *new* default, sin or crime, but for continuing to be, in fault and foible, the very same man in whose faults and foibles he had delighted as a friend.

Then, if the object of the new play be—as all will admit—to present King Harry as our patriotic darling, henceforth Bates and Williams are good enough for him to practise his talk upon, and he may rant about St. Crispin's Day until the lowing herd winds slowly o'er the lea. But he must not be allowed to meet Falstaff. As he once very prettily said of Hotspur—

Two stars keep not their motion in one sphere

and therefore he must not be allowed to meet Falstaff. *For Falstaff can kill him with a look.*

This advances beyond the rejection to an explanation of the death; at the same time it very fairly represents the majority opinion of modern critics, whether muddle-headed or not. Thus if we were to make another foray across the Border and arrive at Glasgow we should find Professor Alexander holding that if Hal's soliloquy is to be regarded as in full dramatic keeping and revelatory of a detached and self-controlled nature then the man who speaks it has no right "to turn without warning on his companions, when it suits him to cast them off, and to point to Falstaff as 'the tutor and the feeder of my riots.' "[15] The conclusion here is that Hal "is not the offspring of the poet's reflection and passion" —from which it would follow (I suppose) that in his trilogy Shakespeare was not very profoundly concerned with working towards an ideal kingship. But at Cambridge again—and finally—we should find Mr. E. M. W. Tillyard declaring the Prince to be indeed Shakespeare's attempt at defining the perfect ruler. And if we incline to sympathise with so dangerous a rebel as Falstaff we are being misled by "the sense of security created in nineteenth-century England by the predominance of the British navy."[16]

7

The little tour we have just concluded should at least give us the main terms of the problem, a problem adumbrated by Nicholas Rowe in 1709 when he wrote of Falstaff:

[Shakespeare] has given him so much Wit as to make him almost too agreeable; and I don't know whether some People have not, in remembrance of the Diversion he had formerly afforded 'em, been sorry to see his Friend

15 P. Alexander, *Shakespeare's Life and Art* (1939), p. 120.
16 E. M. W. Tillyard, *Shakespeare's History Plays* (1944), p. 291.

Hal use him so scurvily, when he comes to the Crown in the End of the
Second Part of *Henry* the Fourth.[17]

The "scurvy" treatment of Falstaff is quite in keeping with a certain
insensibility in the Elizabethans which appears in many gulling scenes
on the stage. But we are liable to feel it not consonant either with
Shakespeare's humanity to a major creation, or with the sympathy and
admiration which must surely be claimed from us for Hal, a character
who is being "groomed" (as the studios say) for the field of Agincourt.
We may now consider more at large certain efforts at a solution of the
problem.

Can we find some light in which the rejection of Falstaff commends
itself to our sympathies while operating wholly within the sphere of
psychological realism? I must say in advance that I think the answer to
be "No." All through the trilogy there are penetrations enough into a
deeper Harry Monmouth, and the rejection can be analysed in terms of
these. But, by and large, I think something profounder is operating here
than Shakespeare's understanding of the son of Henry Bolingbroke.
There are times in all drama when immemorial forces come into play,
and with the end of Falstaff we touch once more what Professor Schück-
ing is fond of calling the limits of Shakespearian realism.

In terms of essential drama Falstaff's rejection and death are very
important—indeed they are the end of the whole business. Falstaff's
corner of *Henry V* is extremely wonderful; the rest is a slack-water play,
stirred here and there by simple patriotic feeling. For comedy now
Shakespeare had so little list that he fell back upon comic Scots, Irish
and Welshmen—the resource, I think I may say, of a professional enter-
tainer hard pressed indeed. Moreover, that the poet of *Romeo and Juliet*
should have executed the wooing of Katharine—that *ne plus ultra* of all
obtuseness—must fill us with dismay until we persuade ourselves (with a
school of critics romantic, no doubt) that there here glints at us from
behind the mask the master's most inscrutable smile. In a word, all this
matter ends for Shakespeare with Falstaff and not with a foreign conquest; and there must be reason for this.

8

And first there is Bradley, whose acknowledgment of the uncomfort-
ableness of the rejection is emphatic.[18] If we have enjoyed the Falstaff
scenes (and Shakespeare surely meant them to be enjoyed), we feel a
good deal of pain and some resentment when Henry first turns upon his
old companion with talk like a clergyman's and then sends back the
Chief Justice to commit him to prison; nor are our regrets diminished

[17] Rowe is cited by A. Shaaber, *2 Henry IV* (a New Variorum Shakespeare), p. 584.
[18] Bradley's essay is in *Oxford Lectures on Poetry*. I have largely employed his own words. . . .

when, in *Henry V,* it is powerfully suggested to us that Falstaff has, in fact, died of wounded affection. Why did Shakespeare end his drama with a scene which, though undoubtedly striking, leaves an impression so unpleasant . . . ?

9

There is so much of suggestion in Bradley's essay that more than one critic has found in it a starting-point for reflections of his own. Thus the germ of Professor Charlton's interpretation is essentially in the notion "that Falstaff's freedom of soul was in part illusory, and that the realities of life refused to be conjured away by his humour"—or in this and an earlier statement of Bradley's that, like no other Shakespearian character, "Falstaff was degraded by Shakespeare himself."

In *The Merry Wives of Windsor* Shakespeare, as it were, reconventionalises Falstaff; turns him so decidedly into a gull and a buffoon that the thing is like a rejection in itself, or a manifesto of complete eventual disinterest in the character. Why does Shakespeare, even more cruelly than Henry, thus trample Falstaff into extinction? Because, Charlton says, Falstaff had let Shakespeare down. Falstaff revealed himself as being not what Shakespeare sought: an adequate comic hero, equipped for the true freedom of the world of comedy. And this letting Shakespeare down seems to have provoked a positive animus in the poet against his creation. Not only did it produce the "ruthless exposure, [the] almost malicious laceration" of the *Merry Wives;* it is the reason why Falstaff was not gently dismissed on some pre-coronation deathbed, but brutally in "a scene which has aroused more repugnance than any other in Shakespeare," and as a result of actions in Henry which are "an offence against humanity, and an offence which dramatically never becomes a skill."

What, then, according to this theory, is that true nature of a comic hero to which Falstaff fails to measure up? Since a comedy is a play which ends happily its hero, we are told, must be

> likely to overcome whatever impediments to his well-being may be presented by the episodes of the play; and these episodes . . . must be representative of the obstacles which, in experience at large, are presented to man in the dilemmas inherent in more or less normal encounters with the world as the world is.

The comic hero, in fact, "must be endowed with the temperament and the arts to triumph over the stresses of circumstance." Now, Falstaff is insatiably curious to provide situations which test or even strain his genius for overcoming them. Mastery of circumstance is his pride—and so superficially he is an incomparable comic hero. But on a deeper view his attitude or philosophy is inadequate to cope with life even within that scope of worldly wisdom which is the philosophy of comedy. In the scene which a mature comedy must contemplate there are forces which Falstaff's measuring-stick cannot measure, and

> the world in which Falstaff's successors in comedy would have to prove their genius for mastery, would necessarily have to be a larger and a richer world than Falstaff's.

Hence Falstaff's failure, and Shakespeare's ruthless writing of him off.

If there is anything in the argument I have earlier advanced—to wit, that the major creations of a dramatist represent so many possible blendings or equilibriums of the abundant raw materials of personality which are his in virtue of his artist's nature—we must regard Charlton's argument as of considerable interest. But whatever be the dynamics of dramatic creation it would surely be extravagant to suggest that the artist's various progeny represent so many tentative essays in self-improvement—the bad shots among which he will then be prompted to "trample into extinction." For the dramatist is quite plainly not seeking about for an exemplar; rather he is like a pagan constructing a pantheon in which there shall be variously reflected the many sides of his own nature; and his satisfaction is simply in creation and in abundance. Thus such a psychological theory as I have hinted at affords no reason to suppose that Shakespeare would be particularly prone to turn upon Falstaff and disown or destroy him. If, on the other hand, we eschew psychology and stick to aesthetics, and with Charlton view Shakespeare's problems simply as one within the theory of comedy, we may believe indeed that Shakespeare might lose interest in Falstaff, but not that he would harry him. And it is just our sense of a persecution that has to be explained. Bradley's is still, perhaps, the best explanation: our having this sense results from Shakespeare's failing of his intention to manœuvre Falstaff into an unsympathetic light. But is there anything more to be said?

10

Obviously, one possibility remains. Shakespeare *succeeded* in manœuvring Falstaff into an unsympathetic light. If, with Bradley, we feel otherwise, we are being sentimental, un-Elizabethan, and disregardful of the fortunes of Falstaff as the drama develops. This is the contention of Professor Dover Wilson.

That Shakespeare himself rejected Falstaff is nonsense, Dover Wilson says; in the Epilogue to *Henry IV* he promised more of him, and if, instead, *Henry V* gave an account of his death this was simply the best way of dealing with the awkward fact that Will Kempe, who created the part, had left the Lord Chamberlain's men. Thus all that falls to be considered is the propriety and dramatic fitness of Henry's dismissing

Falstaff in the way he does. In discussing Falstaff, therefore, Dover Wilson would hold within the bounds of the two parts of *Henry IV;* and his case is that we should mark at once their unity and—more adequately than Bradley—their presentation of a Falstaff who by no means remains the same person throughout. His status changes. As a result of ludicrous deception, and quite without any deserving, he becomes a person of altogether more consideration than he was at first. This rise in his fortunes—from something like "the prince's jester," "an allowed fool" or a "rascally old camp-follower," to one generally supposed the vanquisher of Hotspur—discovers him to be arrogant and overweening; and these traits if they are not obscured to us do in fact alienate our sympathies. Moreover Shakespeare's dramatic intention is perfectly clear if we do not, like Bradley who ignores the serial character of dramatic representation, construct our own portrait of Falstaff almost entirely from the first part of the play. If we really *follow* the play we shall find that though Falstaff's wit grows no less fascinating he comes to inspire less and less affection. And this is enough to render the rejection palatable—always supposing that we remember another relevant fact, to the exposition of which Dover Wilson devotes much space. The story of the Prodigal Prince and his Misleader is, at a certain important level, a Morality. It is the Morality of a Ruler who has to make choice between Vanity and Government; it is "a Tudor version of a time-honoured theme," in which "the forces of iniquity were allowed full play upon the stage, including a good deal of horse-play, provided they were brought to nought, or safely locked up in Hell, at the end." So must not Falstaff, then, be locked up in the Fleet? The fact is that

> the Falstaff-Hal plot embodies a composite myth which had been centuries amaking, and was for the Elizabethans full of meaning that has largely disappeared since then. . . . They [the audience] knew, from the beginning, that the reign of this marvellous Lord of Misrule must have an end, that Falstaff must be rejected by the Prodigal Prince, when the time for reformation came. . . . Prince Hal and Falstaff, for us merely characters in a play, were for the Elizabethans that and a great deal more. They embodied in dramatic form a miscellaneous congeries of popular notions and associations, almost all since gone out of mind, in origin quasi-historical or legendary, pagan and Christian, ethical and political, theatrical, topographical and even gastronomical.

In other words, the Falstaff-Hal story subsumes divers traditional significances for the most part already embodied in drama, and the rejection scene is unexceptionable to an audience aware of and properly balancing these. Thus Falstaff partakes of the character not only of the *miles gloriosus* of Latin comedy, of the Devil of the Miracle Plays, of the Vice of the Moralities, of the traditional boon-companion of Henry, of

the historical Oldcastle and Fastolfe; he partakes too of the character of
Riot in the early Tudor interludes, and in one of these—*The Enterlude
of Youth*—he is quite remarkably paralleled. This little play

> opens with a dialogue between Youth and Charity. The young man, heir
> to his father's land, gives insolent expression to his self-confidence, lustihood,
> and contempt for spiritual things. Whereupon Charity leaves him, and he
> is joined by Riot, that is to say wantonness, who presently introduces him
> to Pride and Lechery. The dialogue then becomes boisterous, and continues
> in that vein for some time, much no doubt to the enjoyment of the audience.
> Yet, in the end, Charity reappears with Humility; Youth repents; and the
> interlude terminates in the most seemly fashion imaginable. . . .
>
> Riot, like Falstaff, escapes from tight corners with a quick dexterity; like
> Falstaff, commits robbery on the highway; like Falstaff, jests immediately
> afterwards with his young friend on the subject of hanging; and like Falstaff,
> invites him to spend the stolen money at a tavern, where, he promises, "We
> will drink diuers wine" and "Thou shalt haue a wench to kysse Whansoeuer
> thou wilte"; allurements which prefigure the Boar's Head and Mistress Doll
> Tearsheet.

Riot, then, "prefigures" Falstaff, and the Tudor attitude to Riot must be
taken into account when we come to consider the discomfiture of the
knight.

What Dover Wilson is really providing here, it might be maintained,
is a sort of second line of defence. As a person, or character in a drama
realistically conceived, Falstaff is gradually so developed that we are
not disturbed at seeing him turned off by another character carefully
developed in terms of the same sort of realistic drama. But if we *are*
disturbed we are to recall that this representation has a sort of abstract
or allegorical quality as well, and fortify ourselves by considering "what
would have followed had the Prince chosen Vanity instead of Government, Falstaff and not the Lord Chief Justice." Is this an illogical way
of tackling the problem, arguing both for the psychological integrity of
the drama and for an overriding myth which the characters must obey?
It seems to me an explanation not much contrary to the logic of the
theatre, where actions and situations have frequently more than one
significance, and where these significances are often at an obscure interplay. Shakespeare's characters, I think, are nearly always real human
beings before they are anything else; but undeniably they *are* at times
something else: they take on the simpler rôles of archetypal drama; and
then there will be "edges" (as the painters say) between generic character and psychological portraiture which the dramatist must cope with,
using what finesse he can. It seems to me, therefore, that Dover Wilson
gets furthest with the problem; and I am only concerned to wonder
whether a further stone or two may yet be added to the edifice he has
raised.

11

Two points would seem to be significant. If Shakespeare does indeed succeed in making the rejection palatable to persons adequately aware of traditional matters lying behind the play, it is yet in the theatre that he does so, for that the thing continues to *read* uncomfortably after all that Dover Wilson has to say I believe there will be few to deny. What does this mean? It means that although Shakespeare doubtless relied on certain contemporary attitudes to Riot and the like, he relied even more on something perennially generated in the consciousness or disposition of an audience in a theatre—whether they belong to Elizabethan times or to our own. And it is here that I would knit the debate on Falstaff to the theme of the present book. For what I have tried to urge is simply this: that in the interpretation of Shakespeare a study of the psychology of poetic drama (which leads us to understand his *medium*) is at least as important as a study of the contemporary climate of opinion (which gives simply *conditions* under which he worked).

The second point concerns the emphatic and wonderful account in *Henry V* of the death of Falstaff. It is all very well for Dover Wilson to point to the promise of more Falstaff made in the Epilogue to *2 Henry IV* and infer that the subsequent death was a matter of mere theatrical convenience. But surely the Epilogue to *Henry IV* is dramatically altogether less authoritative than the account of Falstaff's passing in the later play; and what Shakespeare there wrote appears to me (because it is so wonderful) much less like an expedient dictated by changes in personnel in his company than the issue of his reflections on the inner significance of what had happened at the close of the earlier drama. "The King has kild his heart," says Mistress Quickly as Falstaff lies dying. "The King hath run bad humors on the Knight," says Nym, and Pistol at once responds: "*Nym, thou hast spoke the right, his heart is fracted and corroborate.*" None of these worthies would cut much of a figure in a witness-box; nevertheless there is no mistaking the dramatic function of the three consenting voices. The truth of the matter is summed here; there follows the new king's dexterous, necessary but none too pleasant entrapping of Cambridge, Scroop and Gray; then comes the tremendous account of Falstaff's end—and after that we are set for Agincourt and the regeneration and triumph of England. It is of set purpose, then, that the rejection of Falstaff is so resounding, so like a killing. And the reverberation of that purpose sounds here in *Henry V*. What is it? There is an allegorical purpose, Dover Wilson says, and with this I agree. But I think, too, that among the "notions and associations . . . gone out of mind" embodied in this "composite myth which had been centuries amaking" there conceivably lies something deeper, something which belongs equally with drama and with magic.

When Shakespeare makes Falstaff die "ev'n just betweene Twelve and One, ev'n at the turning o' th' Tyde," he is touching a superstition, immemorial not only along the east coast of England from Northumberland to Kent but in many other parts of the world too—one shared by Dickens's Mr. Peggotty (who speaks of it expressly) and the Haidas on the Pacific coast of North America.[19] But there is more of magic about Falstaff than this; and Dover Wilson, whom the editing of Shakespeare has schooled in a fine awareness of the reverberations of English words, is more than once well on the scent. "How doth the Martlemas, your Master?" Poins asks Bardolph. And Dover Wilson comments:

> Martlemas, or the feast of St Martin, on 11 November, was in those days of scarce fodder the season at which most of the beasts had to be killed off and salted for the winter, and therefore the season for great banquets of fresh meat. Thus it had been for centuries, long before the coming of Christianity. In calling him a "Martlemas" Poins is at once likening Falstaff's enormous proportions to the prodigality of fresh-killed meat which the feast brought, and acclaiming his identity with Riot and Festivity in general.

Falstaff, in fact, is the "sweet beef," "the roasted Manning-tree ox with the pudding in his belly," who reigns supreme on the board of the Boar's Head in Eastcheap—"a London tavern . . . almost certainly even better known for good food than for good drink." There is thus from the first a symbolical side to his vast and genuine individuality; and again and again the imagery in which he is described likens him to a whole larder of "fat meat."

> "Call in Ribs, call in Tallow" is Hal's cue for Falstaff's entry in the first great Boar's Head scene; and what summons to the choicest feast in comedy could be more apt? For there is the noblest of English dishes straightaway: Sir John as roast Sir Loin-of-Beef, gravy and all.

Is it not—I find myself asking—as if the "brawn," Sir John, "the sow that hath overwhelmed all her litter but one," were some vast creature singled out from the herd and dedicated to a high festival indeed? But such festivals commemorate more than the need to reduce stock against a winter season. They commemorate a whole mythology of the cycle of the year, and of sacrifices offered to secure a new fertility in the earth.

Now, anthropologists are always telling us of countries gone waste and barren under the rule of an old, impotent and guilty king, who must be ritually slain and supplanted by his son or another before the saving rains can come bringing purification and regeneration to the land.[20] Is not Henry IV in precisely the situation of this king? Dover

[19] The superstition is noticed by Sir J. G. Frazer, *The Golden Bough* (abridged edition, 1922), p. 35.
[20] See F. M. Cornford, *The Origin of Attic Comedy* (1914), chap. iv, "Some Types of Dramatic Fertility Ritual," sec. 28, "The Young Man and the Old King."

Wilson avers that it is so, without any thought of magical implication:

> . . . his reign and all his actions are overhung with the consciousness . . . of personal guilt . . . a fact that Shakespeare never misses an opportunity of underlining. . . . We see him first at the beginning of act 3 crushed beneath the disease that afflicts his body and the no less grievous diseases that make foul the body of his kingdom.

Perhaps, then, we glimpse here a further reason why the rejection of Falstaff is inevitable—not merely traditionally and moralistically inevitable but symbolically inevitable as well. And this may be why, when in the theatre, we do not really rebel against the rejection; why we find a fitness too in its being sudden and catastrophic. As long as we are in the grip of drama it is profoundly fit that Hal, turning king and clergyman at once, should run bad humours on the knight, should kill his heart. For the killing carries something of the ritual suggestion, the obscure *pathos,* of death in tragedy.

I suggest that Hal, by a displacement common enough in the evolution of ritual, kills Falstaff instead of killing the king, his father. In a sense Falstaff *is* his father; certainly is a "father-substitute" in the psychologist's word; and this makes the theory of a vicarious sacrifice the more colourable. All through the play there is a strong implicit parallelism between Henry Bolingbroke and his policies and Falstaff and *his* policies; and at one point in the play the two fathers actually, as it were, fuse (like Leonardo's two mothers in his paintings of the Virgin and St. Anne), and in the Boar's Head tavern King Falstaff sits on his throne while his son Prince Henry kneels before him. And Falstaff, in standing for the old king, symbolises all the accumulated sin of the reign, all the consequent sterility of the land. But the young king draws his knife at the altar—and the heart of that grey iniquity, that father ruffian, is as fracted and corroborate as Pistol avers. Falstaff's rejection and death are very sad, but Sir James Frazer would have classed them with the Periodic Expulsion of Evils in a Material Vehicle, and discerned beneath the skin of Shakespeare's audience true brothers of the people of Leti, Moa and Lakor.[21]

If this addition of another buried significance to the composite myth of Hal and Falstaff should seem extravagant, or an injudicious striving

---

[21] For Leti, Moa and Lakor see Frazer, op. cit., p. 566. I hope it will be clear that what I am here concerned with is the *multiple* significance of the Falstaff story. To assert that Falstaff "is" the sacrificial object in a fertility ritual is not in the least to deny that he "is" (a good deal less remotely indeed) the Riot of a Morality; nor, again, that he "is" a latent personality of Shakespeare's; nor, yet again, that he "is" an aspect of the human psyche in general. For notice of one interpretation in terms of this last idea I am indebted to Mr. Lionel Trilling's *Freud and Literature,* which cites an essay by Dr. Franz Alexander not available to me as these sheets are passing through the press.

Dr. Alexander undertakes nothing more than to say that in the development of Prince Hal we see the classic struggle of the ego to come to normal adjustment, beginning with the rebellion against the father, going on to the conquest of the super-ego (Hotspur, with after Morgann's "lightness of air," let it be remembered that drama, like religious ritual, plays upon atavic impulses of the mind. All true drama penetrates through representative fiction to the condition of myth. And Falstaff is in the end the dethroned and sacrificed king, the scapegoat as well as the sweet beef. For Falstaff, so Bacchic, so splendidly with the Maenads Doll and Mistress Quickly a creature of the wine-cart and the cymbal, so fit a sacrifice (as Hal early discerns) to lard the lean, the barren earth, is of that primitive and magical world upon which all art, even if with a profound unconsciousness, draws.

his rigid notions of honour and glory), then to the conquest of the *id* (Falstaff, with his anarchic self-indulgence), then to the identification with the father (the crown scene) and the assumption of mature responsibility. An analysis of this sort is not momentous and not exclusive of other meanings.

The last sentence assuredly applies to the various significances that I have endeavoured to educe in the present book. Mr. Trilling's essay (*Horizon*, September, 1947, xvi, 92) is a most valuable treatment of its subject and may usefully be compared with Mr. C. S. Lewis's *Psycho-Analysis and Literary Criticism* (*Essays and Studies*, xxvii, 1941).

ROBERT LANGBAUM

Character versus Action in Shakespeare

THE REINTERPRETATION or, as some critics would have it, the misinter-
pretation of Shakespeare in the nineteenth century is worth reviewing
not only for the light it throws on that elusive thing, the *real* Shakespeare, but also for the light it throws on the difference between the mind
of Europe before and after the Enlightenment. For it is because they
had lost sight of that traditional ethos from which the Enlightenment
separates us that nineteenth-century readers read Shakespeare as they
read the literature of their own time. They read him not as drama in
the traditional Aristotelian sense, not in other words as a literature of
external action in which the events derive meaning from their relation
to a publicly acknowledged morality, but as literature of experience, in
which the events have meaning inasmuch as they provide the central
character with an occasion for experience—for self-expression and self-
discovery. What such a reading suggests is that drama depends for its
structure on belief in a single objective moral system, and dissolves without that belief into monodrama—into the nineteenth century's substitute
for poetic drama, the dramatic monologue.

Thus, the nineteenth-century reading of Shakespeare gives great
weight to the soliloquies, which are just the moments when the point
of view of the central character seems to obliterate the general perspective of the play. The dramatic monologue is largely modelled on the
Shakespearean soliloquy; for in the Shakespearean soliloquy as they read
it, nineteenth-century poets thought they had found the form by which
they could objectify and dramatize their essentially subjective and lyrical
impulse. It is significant, therefore, that in our time, when the effort of
Shakespeare criticism has been to restore to the plays their Elizabethan
ethos, the soliloquies have been alleged to be not characteristic and self-
expressive at all but just those moments when the speaker steps out of
character to make an expository utterance, to speak not for his own particular perspective but for the general perspective of the play.

From *The Poetry of Experience* by Robert Langbaum, pp. 161–164; 167–181. © Copyright
1957 by Robert Langbaum. Reprinted by permission of Random House, Inc. and Chatto
and Windus, Ltd. The article has been somewhat abridged and several footnotes dropped.

As we are nowadays given to understand, Shakespeare's soliloquies are those moments in the play that correspond to the choruses of Greek tragedy, moments when the action stops for narration, moral judgment or general reflection. . . .

The twentieth-century scholarship that has made us aware of this self-descriptive convention in Shakespeare—the convention "whereby the good characters," to quote E. E. Stoll, "speak of themselves frankly as good and the wicked as wicked"[1]—has changed our understanding of Shakespeare's plays by restoring to us the world-view out of which the plays were written. For if, on the one hand, the self-descriptive convention can be considered as merely primitive, as a sign of the still imperfect emergence of the dramatic form from the lyric and narrative, it can also, on the other hand, be considered as the entirely adequate expression of an absolutist world-view. There is surely something deeper involved than a stage convention when the whole imaginative fabric of *Macbeth* is determined by the fact that the two protagonists call their deed a murder and summon up a universe of blood to bear witness against them. "Macbeth and Lady Macbeth themselves call it a murder," Stoll says in his essay on Shakespeare's criminals, "because it is a murder, because public and poet could see it in no other light—not in *their* [the Macbeths'] light, to be sure." "In short," he concludes, "the doctrine of the point of view simply had not arrived. There was as yet no Ibsen in the drama, no Henry James in the novel, no *Ring and the Book.*"

The point of view had not arrived because people had not yet learned, in literature at least, to separate truth from the public view of truth. Though Machiavelli had already broached the idea, it was not yet understood that experience might be categorized according to some other scheme, a scheme by which the same act might be called something other than murder. In other words, the point of view was conceived not as the result of a particular world-view but as a relative position on the moral scale, a scale recognized by hero and villain alike. A case in point is the Elizabethan dramatists' misunderstanding of Machiavelli. Machiavellian characters like Marlowe's Jew of Malta and Shakespeare's Iago announce their villainy, recognize the moral scale by taking for themselves the lowest position on it; whereas Machiavelli had precisely questioned the scale and proposed new virtues according to quite another scale.

Thus, the character in traditional drama cannot be wholly absorbed in his particular perspective, but keeps one eye on the general perspective from which he must take the judgment of his actions. This is the crucial difference that separates us from so much pre-Enlightenment liter-

[1] *Shakespeare Studies* (New York: Macmillan, 1927), p. 102.

ature, causing us to "romantically" misread as the scholars tell us. It is difficult for us to understand the lack of protest among Dante's sufferers in hell, or that Dante's sympathy for Francesca implies no criticism of the Divine judgment against her, or that our sympathy for the fate of the tragic hero ought not to imply criticism of the gods and their ways. Apparently, the moral order was accepted as fixed in a way that we now accept only the natural order; and the combination of suffering and acquiescence was probably the secret of the old tragic emotion—an emotion we talk a good deal about but which always, I suspect, eludes us. For we have been trained to expect the particular perspective to be carried to its logical conclusion in self-justifying values. But the traditional character only half represents himself and half helps to expose the moral meaning of the play. He acts out his own story in order to reinforce the moral order.

It is largely, then, on the soliloquies that the issue hangs between the twentieth-century, anti-psychological interpretation of Shakespeare, as represented by Stoll, and the nineteenth-century psychological interpretation, which is best summed up I think in A. C. Bradley's *Shakespearean Tragedy* (1904). The issue hangs on the soliloquies because dialogue is necessarily characteristic, whereas we have really to choose between reading the soliloquies from a particular or from the general perspective. From a particular perspective, we read the speaker's account as a characteristic distortion; we sympathize but do not believe him, and have therefore to employ intricate psychological concepts of self-deception and subconscious motivation to understand the self-revelation the speaker does not intend. . . . [D]ramatic structure dissolves along with belief in a single objective moral order. For once we stop judging by an external standard, we stop understanding the character by what he does and says. We start understanding him from inside, through sympathy. And once we start sympathizing, the central character is no longer the Aristotelian "agent" of the action but the creator of its meaning. Drama, in other words, gives way to monodrama, to the dramatic monologue.

Sympathy would seem to have been responsible in the first place for the psychological interpretation of Shakespeare, and it is no coincidence that the new interpretation made its first appearance in the latter eighteenth century when we note the decline of the dogmatic and the beginning of the sympathetic or humanitarian attitude. Our reading of a Hamlet soliloquy depends, after all, on whether we give more emphasis to Hamlet's moral problem or to his experience in facing the problem. If the moral imperative is uppermost in our minds, we are likely to agree with Hamlet when he chides his delay; we are likely to be concerned with his delinquency and to hope that his confession of guilt will advance him toward the fulfilment of his duty. But if we do not find the moral imperative compelling, we are likely to be less concerned with Hamlet's guilt than with his suffering from the sense of guilt; and we are likely to hope not so much that he will do his duty as that he will free himself from the sense of guilt. Nor will the uncompelling moral imperative strike us as a sufficient motive for so much suffering; in which case we will seek out an underlying motive, less abstract and external, more psychological and even biological, more consonant in other words with our assumptions about the mainsprings of human action. An abstract morality lurking in the dim periphery of our attention can hardly compete with the vivid human being filling the stage. Or to put it conversely, where dogmatic sanction recedes, sympathy rushes in to fill the vacuum.

Modern sympathy is even better illustrated when we see it turned upon Shakespeare's villains, for there it is clearly at odds with the plot. All the subtleties of nineteenth-century Iago criticism are attempts to account for the fact that, in spite of Iago's villainy, we find him attractive. We admire him because he has a strong and clearly defined point of view, and we sympathize with him because he is on the stage and claims our attention. To the extent that he is there to be understood, we try to understand him; we give him our sympathy as a primary condition anterior to judgment.

Iago was *understood* in the traditional interpretation as well, but he was understood as congruent with his moral category. When the moral imperative is, however, less compelling than the sheer appeal of the human being on the stage, sympathy overflows the weakened confines of the moral category; so that the modern reader finds in Iago a life that exceeds the moral category and is not to be accounted for by it. The modern interest—what we mean by *character* in fact—is in just that which is incongruent with the moral category. The modern reader can sympathize with any character, regardless of his moral position in the plot, provided only that he is sufficiently central to claim our attention, and has a sufficiently definite point of view and sufficient power of intellect and will to hold our interest. Thus, sympathy is likely to be more important than moral judgment in the modern interpretation not only of Iago but also of Shakespeare's Richard III, Macbeth, Shylock and Falstaff, and Marlowe's Tamburlaine, Faustus and Jew of Malta. If we have no sympathy for the execrable Aaron of Shakespeare's *Titus Andronicus*, it is not because he is wicked but because he is too crude and stupid to command our interest. Where we do find Elizabethan villains attractive, it is in the same sense and for the same reason that we admire Browning's duke in *My Last Duchess*.

We know how the decline of the moral sanctions against Jews and usurers has, by turning our sympathy toward Shylock, turned *The Merchant of Venice* from a crude comedy into a pathetic if not tragic drama; and how the modern audience, unable to keep uppermost in its mind a distinct idea of the social limitations Malvolio has violated in daring to aspire to a Lady's hand, soon begins to feel sorry for him. Since the comic effect depends specifically on the exclusion of sympathy, it is even more important in comedy than in tragedy that we keep the offended mores in mind—which is why fewer comedies than tragedies survive, and why the comedies that do survive do so through the pathetic or psychological interest that modern readers think they find there.

Falstaff's comic effect has not been impaired. But that is because his comic role has been made philosophical by the modern elevation of his character, an elevation which Stoll attributes to the decline of the chivalric code of honour. We laugh with Falstaff when he makes the common-sense attack upon honour ("Can honour set to a leg?"), because we see him as the witty philosopher of a rival world-view. But according to Stoll, the Elizabethans laughed at him for his transparent attempt to justify his cowardice. They saw him as a self-describing coward turning the general perspective against himself by poking sarcastic fun at himself. Stoll even suggests that Falstaff might have winked at the audience as he "descanted on the duty of discretion."[2] Such humorous self-betrayal would have been no more unpsychological than the startling self-betrayal of Shakespeare's villains in the tragedies.

But whether or not we are willing to go along with Stoll on this point (there is, after all, reason to believe that the laugh on chivalry had begun by Shakespeare's time), the issue between the psychological and anti-psychological interpretations of Falstaff is whether as coward, lecher and glutton he is the butt of the comedy and deservedly outwitted in the end; or whether he is the maker of the comedy, playing the butt for the sake of the humour which he turns upon himself as well as everyone else—whether he is, in other words, victorious in all the wit combats whatever his circumstantial defeat. It is essentially the issue of Hamlet and Macbeth criticism, whether they confront their difficulties or create them; and of Iago criticism, whether he is the villain or as maker of the plot merely playing the villain. In other words, are the characters agents of the plot with only as much consciousness as the plot requires; or have they a residue of intelligence and will beyond what the plot requires and not accounted for by it, so that they stand somehow above the plot, conscious of themselves inside it? The latter view assumes that we can apprehend more about the characters than the plot tells us, assumes our sympathetic apprehension of them.

The Falstaff question has been only less important than the Hamlet question in establishing the psychological interpretation of Shakespeare.

2 *Shakespeare Studies,* p. 468.

Both Hamlet and Falstaff began to appear in their new complex and enigmatic character in the 1770's, the decade of Werther and of a European Wertherism that owed much to an already well-established sentimental tradition in England. Of such a propitious age for psychological criticism, Maurice Morgann, the projector of the new Falstaff, was one of the advanced spirits—liberal in politics, humanitarian in sentiment, and in literature endowed with the new sensibility.

Morgann's sensibility is abundantly illustrated in the *Essay on the Dramatic Character of Sir John Falstaff* (1777), where the perceptions are far in advance of the dialectic. It is his fundamental sympathy for Falstaff that Morgann is trying to explain when he undertakes to prove that, in spite of cowardly actions, "Cowardice *is not* the *Impression*, which the *whole* character of *Falstaff* is calculated to make on the minds of an unprejudiced [i.e. sympathetic] audience." And it is on the ground of experience that he makes the novel distinction between our "*mental Impressions*" and our "*Understanding*" of character—whereby "we often condemn or applaud characters and actions on the credit of some logical process, while our hearts revolt, and would fain lead us to a very different conclusion." The "Understanding" takes cognizance, he says, of "*actions* only," and from these infers "*motives* and *character;* but the sense we have been speaking of proceeds in a contrary course, and determines of *actions* from certain *first principles of character,* which seem wholly out of the reach of the Understanding."

Unfortunately, Morgann is a bit frightened by the revolutionary nature of his case, and tries to prove it to his eighteenth-century readers on their own rationalistic and moral grounds. His essay is therefore valuable for its scattered insights rather than for the hair-splitting, text-citing argument destructive of the dramatic and comic context which he employs in order to uncover in the *actions* he says do not *matter* evidences of Falstaff's courage. It would have required the dialectical equipment of the next century for Morgann to have granted the moral case against Falstaff and accounted for his sympathetic *impression* of him by quite another order of value. Yet the other order of value is certainly implied by Morgann's distinction between the *first principles* of character which we apprehend sympathetically and its manifestations which we judge. It is also implied by his distinction between "*Constitutional Courage*" and the "Courage founded upon *principle.*" The latter is moral courage, which comes of conformity to "the prevailing modes of honour, and the fashions of the age." But the former is an existential courage, which "extends to a man's whole life, makes a part of his nature, and is not to be taken up or deserted like a mere Moral quality."

It follows—though Morgann does not specifically articulate the conclusion—that our judgment of Falstaff's moral courage must be problematical because based on a shifting idea of honour; whereas our apprehension of his *constitutional* courage must be certain because based on what he is in himself. Only the double apprehension of character could have given rise to Morgann's perception that character may be incongruous with action, that "the *real* character of *Falstaff* may be different from his *apparent* one," and that an author may give wit, dignity and courage to a character made to seem ridiculous, ignoble and cowardly by all external appearances. The recognition that our *impressions* of a character and even of certain of the character's sentiments and actions may be contradictory of his moral category yet "we know not why, natural," leads to the essential method of all psychological criticism in that it compels us "to look farther, and examine if there be not something more in the character than is *shewn*."

Now it is just the habit in Shakespeare criticism of looking for more than is shown that makes Stoll see red, since he contends that this is to treat the character as historical and that there can be no more in a fictitious character than *is* shown. It is true enough that psychological criticism treats the character as though he had a life of which the action presents only a portion; yet Stoll defines the issue, I think, inadequately. For if we conceive the play as larger than the plot, the part of character uncovered by psychological criticism falls not outside the play but outside the moral categories of the plot. The plot, which we understand through moral judgment, becomes a clearing in the forest; while the play shades off to include the penumbra of forest fringe out of which the plot has emerged, a penumbra which we apprehend through sympathy. Such a conception makes room for psychological criticism by dissolving the limits of character and of the play, by suggesting that the limits are always in advance of comprehension. That is how we come by the modern idea of a masterpiece as an enigma whose whole meaning can never be formulated. Comprehension becomes an unending process, historical and evolutionary; while the play itself moves inviolate down the ages, eluding final formulation yet growing, too, in beauty and complexity as it absorbs into its meaning everything that has been thought and felt about it.

According to this conception, Morgann remains within the play, though outside the categories of the plot, when he undertakes to justify Falstaff by an order of value contradictory of his moral position as comic butt outwitted in the end. The *first principles* of character from which we gain our favourable *impression* of Falstaff are those "qualities of a strong mind, particularly Courage and ability," which attract us in spite of the character's vices. They are sufficient to "discharge that *disgust* which arises from vicious manners; and even to attach us . . . to the cause and subject of our mirth with some degree of affection." But a character without courage and ability cannot long command our interest. That is why Morgann can grant all the other vices attributed to Falstaff, but not cowardice: if we "reckon cowardice among his other defects, all the intelligence and wit [i.e. *ability*] in the world could not support him through a single play." The issue is not moral, it is not that coward-ice is the gravest sin; rather it would seem to be whether Falstaff is to exist at all. He is "saturated," says Morgann, "with every folly and with every vice not destructive of his essential character," with every vice, in other words, except cowardice and stupidity which would be destructive. "Courage and Ability are first principles of Character, and not to be destroyed whilst the united frame of body and mind continues whole and unimpaired; they are the pillars on which he stands firm in spight of all his vices and disgraces."

But in what sense is cowardice destructive of character, when there are after all cowardly characters (Shakespeare's Parolles, Jonson's Bobadil)? Morgann's meaning can, I think, be understood in the terms we have established in this discussion. Courage and ability are necessary if Falstaff is to exist as a *character* in the modern sense, as something more than agent of the plot or representative of a moral category—as a pole for sympathy, with a consciousness in excess of the plot's require-ments and a life outside the plot and proof against its accidents. The plot makes him out a coward, "but that is nothing," says Morgann, "if the character itself does not act from any consciousness of this kind, and if our Feelings take his part, and revolt against our understanding." I take this to mean that Falstaff's intention is not to escape danger but to provide humour; just as in the psychological interpretation Iago's intention is to create the plot, and Hamlet's and Macbeth's to exercise their moral sensibility. To entertain so radical an idea, we must have apprehended in these characters a residue of consciousness which is as much a spectator of the action as we are, this consciousness being pre-cisely the quality we apprehend through sympathy.

The fact that our *feelings* should have occasion to revolt against our *understanding* means that we judge this residue of consciousness by an order of value other than moral. Morgann's *courage* and *ability* are existential virtues, virtues which make for the sheer survival of the personality apart from any moral purpose toward which the personality is directed. He speaks at length of the indestructible nature of Falstaff, who, unlike Parolles and Bobadil, is never defeated and never even loses stature from his several disgraces. That is because the disgraces, like the "ill habits, and the accidents of age and corpulence, are no part of his essential constitution . . . they are second natures, not *first*." Falstaff's *first* nature is the "substance of his character [which] remains unim-paired," for "*Falstaff* himself has a distinct and separate subsistence."

Falstaff's courage, remember, is not moral but *constitutional*. It is not Hotspur's kind of courage. It is too bad that Morgann did not under-take the contrast with Hotspur, for it holds good under his interpretation—not to be sure as between cowardice and heroism, but as between two kinds of heroism. If Hotspur is the chivalric hero, Falstaff is the natural hero, the Hero of Existence. His is the courage to be himself, to realize his individuality. He is a hero because of his hard core of character, his fierce loyalty to himself, because he is more alive than other people. By this peculiarly modern reading, Falstaff and Hotspur would represent opposite kinds of heroism both of which go down to defeat; while the Prince, who temporizes between the two extremes, appropriating from each the virtues he can turn to his advantage, becomes prudence triumphant.

Although the eighteenth century could not supply the concepts and vocabulary by which Falstaff might be called a hero, Morgann is already dealing in the distinctive virtues of the new heroism when he attacks as mere prudence the moral virtues Falstaff lacks, and glorifies Falstaff on the ground of his imprudence.

> It may not possibly be wholly amiss to remark in this place, that if Sir *John Falstaff* had possessed any of that Cardinal quality, Prudence, alike the guardian of virtue and the protector of vice; that quality, from the possession or the absence of which, the character and fate of men in this life take, I think, their colour, and not from real vice or virtue; if he had considered his wit, not as *principal* but *accessary* only; as the instrument of power, and not as power itself; . . . he might, without any other essential change, have been the admiration and not the jest of mankind.

Without using the word, the passage effectively describes Falstaff as a hero in the new sense; it contains in brief the whole ethical attitude of the next century. The attack on prudence is the beginning of the romantic ethics. Hypocrisy (the denial of one's own nature) is its worst sin, sincerity (another name for existential courage) its prime virtue. Morgann's Falstaff has the virtues Blake was to recommend in *The Marriage of Heaven and Hell*: "Prudence is a rich, ugly old maid courted by Incapacity," "He who desires but acts not, breeds pestilence," "The road of excess leads to the palace of wisdom." *Excess* explains Falstaff's nature; his girth, his appetites, his laughter, even his style of wit and the rich redundancy of his language—all derive their character from excess; yet they are not for that reason vices, as they would be according to the Aristotelian ethics of the Golden Mean. According to the new ethics, Falstaff's excesses are at once the cause of his failure and of his distinction.

For he commits what Shelley was to call the "generous error," the error of those who try to live life by a vision of it, thus transforming the world about them and impressing upon it their character. This is the secret of Falstaff's appeal. His vision of life takes over whenever he is on the stage; and everyone on stage with him, most notably the Prince, is drawn into his characteristic atmosphere. The only characters who resist his influence are those who, like the King and Hotspur, never confront him. Yet Falstaff's genius for creating his own environment is dangerous, since the single vision of life cannot be identical with reality and must eventually collide with it. That is why the "generous error" distinguishes the Hero of Existence from what Shelley calls the "trembling throng," who "languish" and are "morally dead," who live eclectically because they have not the courage to live out the implications of their own natures, who are too prudent to venture all on what must turn out to have been a noble delusion.[3]

Dr Johnson, who saw where Morgann's kind of criticism was leading, said of him: "Why, Sir, we shall have the man come forth again; and as he has proved Falstaff to be no coward, he may prove Iago to be a very good character."[4] Johnson thought he was indulging in witty hyperbole, but the admiration for Falstaff was in fact to be accompanied in the next century by an admiration for Iago and for all characters alive enough to take over the scene, to assert their point of view as the one through which we understand the action. The new existential rather than moral judgment of character was to dissolve dramatic structure by denying the authority of the plot—making the psychologically read play, like the dramatic monologue, depend for its success upon a central character with a point of view definite enough to give meaning and unity to the events, and the strength of intellect, will and passion, the imaginative strength, to create the whole work before our eyes, to give it a thickness and an atmosphere, an inner momentum, a life.

It is, however, in the isolation of character from plot that we can best see the psychological interpretation of Shakespeare as dissolving dramatic structure and leading us toward the dramatic monologue. For in concentrating on the part of character in excess of plot requirements, and in claiming to apprehend more about character than the plot reveals, the psychological interpretation isolates character from the external motivation of plot (such as money, love, power). It makes of character an autonomous force, motivated solely by the need for self-expression. The psychological interpretation of Falstaff rests, for example, on the assumption that Falstaff does not employ his wit for practical advantage, that he makes no secret of his true nature and therefore does not really expect to deceive the other characters but merely to draw them into his jests. Deny this assumption as Stoll does, and you have a Falstaff who menaces the other characters and vies for advantage in the same way as the rival factions of the play's historical episodes. Such a Falstaff must be judged morally and laughed at as a base clown who is deservedly humiliated and outwitted at every turn.

---

[3] See the Preface to *Alastor* and the last stanza of *Adonais*.
[4] James Boswell, *The Life of Samuel Johnson, LL.D.* (London: J. M. Dent, 1901), III, 230.

But Morgann's Falstaff employs his wit not as the "instrument of power" but as "power itself." And Hazlitt's Falstaff is less interested in sensual gratification than in his own "ideal exaggerated description" of the life of sensuality and freedom, of a world-view he has taken it upon himself to dramatize.

> His pulling out the bottle in the field of battle is a joke to shew his contempt for glory accompanied with danger, his systematic adherence to his Epicurean philosophy in the most trying circumstances. Again, such is his deliberate exaggeration of his own vices, that it does not seem quite certain whether the account of his hostess's bill, found in his pocket, with such an out-of-the-way charge for capons and sack with only one halfpennyworth of bread, was not put there by himself as a trick to humour the jest upon his favourite propensities, and as a conscious caricature of himself. He is represented as a liar, a braggart, a coward, a glutton, &c. and yet we are not offended but delighted with him; for he is all these as much to amuse others as to gratify himself. He openly assumes all these characters to shew the humorous part of them. . . . In a word, he is an actor in himself almost as much as upon the stage, and we no more object to the character of Falstaff in a moral point of view than we should think of bringing an excellent comedian, who should represent him to the life, before one of the police offices.[5]

Falstaff has no motive other than to exercise his genius for comedy. . . .

The effectiveness of character is made to depend on its inaccessibility to the rational and moral categories of the plot. Falstaff, Hamlet and Iago are geniuses whose only purpose is to express their genius. They are creators of the play who must be judged not as we judge men of action but as we judge artists, by the virtuosity of their creations. It matters less whether they are right than that they accomplish what they set out to be and do—that Falstaff conquer with his wit, that Hamlet gain spiritual ascendancy through his moving and profound exploration of moral experience, and that Iago's intrigue be bold, ingenious and successful.

Such a theory is in its ultimate implication destructive of drama. It destroys the play as an entity distinct from its parts, having a logic, meaning and unity of its own to which the parts are subordinated; for it destroys the objective principles which relate the events and characters to each other and to the whole. By leaving events subject to the will of character, it destroys the logic inherent in the events themselves. And by giving unconditional sympathy to sheer vividness of character, it destroys the moral principle which apportions sympathy among the characters according to their deserts. It leaves an anarchic free-for-all in which the characters compete for a sympathy that depends on the ability to command attention, with the strongest character able to assert his point of view against the general meaning.

[5] *Characters of Shakespear's Plays*, pp. 190–91.

What such a theory does is to break down the barriers that hold sympathy in check, subordinating it to the general meaning. It allows sympathy to become a law unto itself, the law of dramatic structure in fact; so that we no longer have the logical unit Aristotle spoke of, with its beginning, middle and end, but rather a succession of whatever characters and events happen to fall within the purview of the character who has captured our sympathy. Instead of a play which is complete because of the working out of its own logic, we have a play whose limits are defined only by the perspective of a central character. Hence the controversy between the anti-psychological critics, who insist that there is only as much character as appears in the play, and the psychological critics, who insist that dramatic characters can be treated as though they were historical, that it is legitimate to speculate upon their lives before and after the play. The question is whether the character is part of a definitive unit, the play; or whether the play is merely an episode in the character's career, an episode whose beginning and end shades off into the rest of his biography. To the extent that perspective replaces logical completeness as the principle of organization, we are moving away from drama toward the dramatic monologue.

There has always been in drama a certain tension between the point of view of each character and the play's final meaning which assigns values to the points of view. And among the audience there has been a corresponding tension between the inclination to be interested in each character out of sheer curiosity and the necessity to judge the characters morally. But character has always given way in drama to general meaning; whereas the nineteenth century preferred to weight the balance in the other direction, to allow the individual point of view and the inclination to be interested in it to have their way against the general meaning. That is what the nineteenth century did with its reading of Shakespeare, where it may not have had the right to, and what it did where it undoubtedly had the right—with its own literature, as in the dramatic monologue.

The dramatic monologue brings to the surface what is underground in drama; what in drama resists the law of the form becomes the law of the dramatic monologue. The sympathy which pulls against the meaning of drama is the meaning and whole *raison d'être* of the dramatic monologue. External and moral relations are still there, but pushed off-stage; they are now the underground and resisting element, the foil against which meaning defines itself. For the meaning of the dramatic monologue derives not from the absorption of the particular in the general but from the defiance of the general. The meaning is not the law which puts character in its place; the meaning *is* character in its unformulated being, in all its particularity.

E. E. STOLL

Henry V[1]

SHAKESPEARE's *Henry V* is the last of his English "histories," which cover the line of kings from Richard II to Richard III. Though itself not one of his greatest plays, it was written, in 1599, when Shakespeare had entered into the plenitude of his powers, had almost finished his series of comedies, and was about to touch the pinnacle of his art in *Hamlet, Othello, King Lear,* and *Macbeth.* That—from 1602 to about 1607—was the period of tragedy; this, of history and comedy; that, the period of gloom and terror; this, of love and joy and "high, heroic things." Not that the prevailing mood of either period is necessarily to be taken for the mood of Shakespeare the man. A man who writes tragedy may himself be not uncheerful, just as one has been known to write jokes for the newspapers at a time when his heart was breaking. But so far as the plays themselves are concerned, the period which ends with *Henry V* and *Twelfth Night* reflects a joy in life and an exuberance of spirits, which then, for some reason, suddenly pass away. This is true not only of the substance but of the style. The expression now is highly colored, lavish of poetry and the beauty of phrase and figure. In the great tragedies ornament seems to be disdained, and the sweetness of the master's style is sometimes almost lost in its Titanic strength.

To this more human and genial period *Henry V* wholly belongs. In it are mingled the serious and the comic, as in *Henry IV*, and the shadow of Fate nowhere appears. Shakespeare is here following the older tradition of the English "history," though much improving upon it. Marlowe, in his *Edward II* (*ca.* 1592), had eliminated the comic element; and Shakespeare, in *Richard III* and *Richard II,* had followed suit.

Reprinted by special permission from *English Readings—Shakespeare's Henry V*, edited by Elmer Edgar Stoll and Martin B. Rudd, Copyright 1922 by Holt, Rinehart and Winston, Inc. [The version that appears here incorporates various changes made by Mr. Stoll for the reprinting of the essay in *Poets and Playwrights* (University of Minnesota Press, 1930). It has been slightly cut.]

1 This essay [was] originally the introduction to an edition of the play published by Messrs. Henry Holt and Co. . . . . here and there certain adjustments and allusions were introduced for a special occasion, a reading before the Shakespeare Association, at Kings College, London, in 1921, shortly after the settlement of the Irish troubles under Mr. Lloyd George.

These "histories" are really tragedies; and both have the pomp and (the earlier, at least) the horror of the older Elizabethan tragic manner. There is the supernatural machinery of the plot, inherited from the tragic poet Seneca—Fate lowering in the background, ghosts shrieking in the foreground, and omens and premonitions, prophecies and curses, fulfilled to the last jot and tittle. And there are atrocious crimes and deeds of violence, and fierce men and comparatively fiercer women, with long high-flown speeches in their mouths, passionate, declamatory, full of introspection and self-consciousness, and often not very closely fitted to the business in hand.

In *Henry IV* and *Henry V*, then, Shakespeare turned back somewhat from the Marlowesque history to the earlier popular tragi-comedy, but he pretty much abandoned the Senecan tragic machinery to be found in both. There were no doubt several reasons for this. In the first place, he must have felt that this tragic manner was too stiff and heavy for some of the material in English history which he wished to present. Henry IV was too businesslike, Hotspur too high-souled and eccentric, to lend himself to such a style. In the second place, he inclined to hearken to the popular cry. Before Marlowe English audiences had delighted in tragedy (or history) blended with comedy, just as they had done in the Middle Ages; such had always been the popular dramatic taste; and Shakespeare instinctively knew that only by satisfying this deep-seated craving could the artistic miracle be wrought—when, as with an electric shock, artist and public come vitally in contact. How then could he meet the popular demand without stooping to it? One of the readiest ways was to drop the portentous and atrocious old tragic manner and adopt one that more nearly accommodated itself to the sobriety and simplicity of life as we know it. Titans and ogres and men heroically mounted on stilts do not mingle readily with jolly good fellows and clowns: you cannot always be sure which set you are meant to laugh at. In *Henry IV* the serious part blends with the comic much more readily than in *Titus Andronicus* or *King John,* if for no other reason, simply because it is more within human reach and compass. And, in the third place, he now wished to treat a subject which demanded this blending of the comic and the serious, of low life and high life, by its very nature. Henry V combined the two elements in his single self. The hero of Agincourt had in life, as in Shakespeare's previous play, been a madcap and boon companion. To the popular heart this was the most interesting thing about his character—on the popular stage it was the one thing that could not be omitted or ignored. In these plays, then, in which he appears, *Henry IV* and *Henry V*, comedy was essential; and to harmonize with the comedy, as well as to fit the historical subject, the serious part must step down a bit to a more human level.

The greatest success in "history" that Shakespeare attained was in the

First Part of Henry IV. Here is to be found his liveliest and most richly-colored picture of tavern and country; here is to be found Falstaff, and Falstaff at his best; and here, in Hotspur, and in young Harry roused to emulation, are to be found a pair of Shakespeare's most radiant figures of English youth and chivalry. But the main thing is that the two elements, serious and comic, hold together better here than in *Henry V*. The Prince of Wales still belongs to both worlds; and both worlds, that is, the court and the Boar's Head in Eastcheap, are made to reflect or echo one another. At court, for instance, Henry IV complains of his son's debauchery and takes him to task; at the Boar's Head, the actual scene between them is enacted by the Prince and Falstaff in burlesque; and then the alarm of war breaks in upon that haunt of jollity, and brings it and the court together, driving the droll and motley crew to Shrewsbury, not in quest of honor, to be sure, though young Harry—roused from his indifference—is in quest of nothing else.

1.

In *Henry V* the hero has already forsaken Eastcheap for ever; Falstaff and his companions he has banished from his sight; and though after Falstaff's death his scurvy cronies follow the army into France, they do not enter the King's presence or indeed have much to do with his story. They are in the play, not so much because they belong there, as because, having been in the play preceding, they might be expected to be in this—the audience craving, like the clientèle of the present-day newspaper, the comic characters it already knows; and because the introduction of new comic characters, more closely connected with the King, had been made difficult by his reformation.

Plot, indeed, is not the strong point of this "history." *Henry V* is, as has been said, rather a series of tableaux. The choruses, which not only effect the transitions but also introduce glowing descriptions, elsewhere out of place, indicate as much. Pictures of life, interspersed with poetry and eloquence—these make up the story. A drama, of course, requires a struggle; and the King, by his reform, is past that. His career is simply a triumphal progress from Harfleur to Agincourt, and from Agincourt on to the French crown and the French princess' hand. There is even no external struggle, because there must be, in this patriotic drama, no enemy able to withstand him.

Wherein, then, lies the value of the drama? In the quality of the pictures of life and character, on the one hand; and in the quality of the eloquence and poetry—the patriotic passion which runs through the play —on the other. It is the latter, the patriotic fervor, along with the dominant figure of the King, that gives the play unity of effect. Nowhere else in Shakespeare is there so much of it as here. John of Gaunt's great speech in *Richard II,*—and that is no more than a speech—is the only thing to compare with it. Shakespeare in general was not so patriotic, or at least not so imperialistic, as his contemporaries Sidney, Raleigh, Spenser, Daniel, and Drayton; he was not interested in America, or "Virginia," as they were, or in the greatness of England there, or in Europe, or on the sea. He had nothing to say, as they had, of the Queen, and the glory of her arms, the vast empire that then was making. He was not highly patriotic, just as he was not a partisan, whether in matters of state or of church. He loved men, loved Englishmen, more than England. But, as he always did, he rose to the occasion: he was enough in love with everything to do that. The choruses and the King's speeches to his soldiers stir and quicken your blood, and ring in your memory, after the book has been laid down:

> Once more unto the breach, dear friends, once more,
> Or close the wall up with our English dead.
> .   .   .   .   .   And you, good yeomen,
> Whose limbs were made in England, show us here
> The mettle of your pasture.

The words thrill us, who in these years have but sat at home, now more than ever, for we know that they were read and uttered of late by thousands of Englishmen on French soil, facing this time, happily, a different foe. Like the words of the Prayer-book and of the devotional parts of the Bible, they have been made sacred by the lips, now silent, which repeated them. Like those, they have become part of the litany of the nation, and of her daughter nations too.

2.

Apart from this, the play interests us most as a picture of life and character. The patriotism, though ardent, is not highly enlightened. The war is for no good cause; Henry's claim to the throne is, for all that he believes in it, unfounded. And the ideal of the English is, so far as it is expressed, honor and glory, not love of country, or liberty, or devotion to one's faith. It is a feudal, chivalric war, waged, not for a cause like a crusade, but like a tournament for a victor's crown. Henry, before the action, rejoices that Englishmen are not there in greater numbers, partly indeed, because "if we are mark'd to die we are enow to do our country loss"; but much more because "the fewer men, the greater share of honour." Henry has the mind of a king but the soul of a paladin. He speaks for the moment the language of knight-errantry, —the language of Sidney, Raleigh, and Drake, to be sure, and all very noble and glorious, but in these days, when bloodshed is of itself more abhorrent, exceedingly remote. For the ethics of statecraft and warfare were, in Shakespeare's time, not so clearly and soundly established as today. English rulers then were a little like some Continental ones of late, and apart from the motive of honor, they were for war from motives of calculating expediency. Henry IV is made by Shakespeare twice to express the opinion of the poet's friend, the Earl of Essex, that peace and unity at home were to be secured by waging foreign wars. In *Henry V* even the Archbishop advises waging one in order to save the endowments of the Church. Like some of the political leaders and writers of late, war they thought the great domestic curative and tonic. And like these, Englishmen then, as well as other Europeans, believed in waging a war of terror. The historical Henry V was no lamb, though he was not quite the lion that Shakespeare makes of him, roaring before the gates of Harfleur:

> If I begin the battery once again,
> I will not leave the half-achieved Harfleur
> Till in her ashes she lies burièd.
> The gates of mercy shall be all shut up,
> And the flesh'd soldier, rough and hard of heart,
> In liberty of bloody hand shall range
> With conscience wide as hell, mowing like grass
> Your fresh fair virgins and your flow'ring infants.
>   (Act III, iii, 7–14.)

His bark is worse than his bite, we trust; but even so his words are not out of keeping with the gentle poet Edmund Spenser's views on the subjugation of Ireland; or with the Spanish ways in Holland—and the Catholic ways in France—of stamping out heresy and dissent; or with the policy of the strong arm and violence as taught by the teacher and mentor of our contemporary Professor Treitschke and General Bernhardi —Niccolò Machiavelli—less than a century before Shakespeare's day.

But Shakespeare was not a political or moral theorist. He was not a theorist at all, not even, in any abstract or analytic sense of the word, a thinker. He was an artist, which is something widely different. His morals and his politics, his science and his history, were those of his time or one still earlier; but his art was for the ages. He was not a philosopher, a seer, an oracle, as some worshippers have taken him to be; he was not, of course, a prophet living in spirit in the nineteenth century while working in the sixteenth; but he was a man and dramatist as others were—Sophocles, Molière, Lope de Vega—and as such he was not very different from a great painter, sculptor, or musician. Like theirs, his work was to reveal not truth but beauty, to imitate and ennoble life, not analyze or expound it. Plot and situation, dialogue and character, style and meter,—these are the elements of his art in which he wrought as he strove to produce the illusion of life upon the stage. These are the things that we should attend to as we, in turn, strive to discover how far he succeeded in producing the illusion of life upon the stage. And in this particular play, as we have seen, plot and situation count for little, dialogue and characters for nearly all.

3.

Chief of the characters is, of course, the King. He is, on the whole, done according to historical and popular tradition; he is the Hal of *Henry IV*, reclaimed and sobered. He has the manliness, the physical strength and ability, the personal courage, the generalship, the ruthlessness (as well as the mercifulness toward the poor and the weak), the piety (though not the bigotry and intolerance), and the exalted patriotic temper, which the chronicler Holinshed had attributed to the great popular hero of the land. But the mere transcription of traits will not go far towards making a character; and Shakespeare gave him many other features, and put in his nostrils the breath of life besides.

The most remarkable thing about him is the way that Shakespeare reforms him and yet contrives to keep him human and recognizable. Reformations are ticklish things to handle on the stage; edifying, but alienating, they ordinarily lead beyond the province of art and poetry into the dry and sterile air of morals or the dank atmosphere of sentimentality. This on the whole the royal reformation does not do. Henry is a knight and a hero, a king and a wise ruler, and a general who has put almost all petty personal considerations under his feet; but he is still a friendly good fellow, has his joke before battle and in the midst of battle, and woos the French princess in no silken terms of gallantry, but more like a captain of cavalry than a king, though more like a king than a suitor, with fire in his heart though with a twinkle in his eye. Wine, at times, is still a bit too good for him; like his princely younger self, he has now and then a longing for the poor creature, small beer. Bardolph, Pistol, and Falstaff himself, risen from the dead, would have known him, though to recall him and what he had been to them, both in purse and in person, would now have cost them a pang. There is in the hero of Agincourt that mixture of the serious and the humorous, of the dignified and the simple and naïve, which was impossible in French tragedy until it came, in the nineteenth century, under Shakespeare's own influence, but which, in some form, is to be found in many of his best characters and is one of the most authentic signs of their reality. They are not mere rôles—not wraiths which the moon shines through.

Some readers may object a little to Henry's obtrusive morality and his familiarity with the Most High. They may be reminded of later czars and kaisers, likewise engaged in wars of aggression, and be inclined to call it all hypocrisy or official cant. Shakespeare surely did not mean it so; the Elizabethans would not have taken it so; and such monarchs, again, like their parties, are specimens of times and manners, now long out of date, but not out of date in the age of Elizabeth. In any case, Shakespeare has deliberately brushed away much of the piety clinging to him in Holinshed. He has added, to be sure, the prayer the night before the battle, in which he speaks of King Richard's death. But that really is a relief; Henry is not so pious as penitent, and would make amends for his father's wrong, by which he profits. And a striking positive change is made when the action is about to begin. The speech he now utters (IV, iii, 18–67), part of which has been quoted above, is all of honor; but the corresponding passage in Holinshed has something of the twang and snuffle of a Puritan preacher's cant:

> But if we should fight in trust of multitude of men, and so get the victorie (our minds being prone to pride), we should thereupon peradventure ascribe the victorie not so much to the gift of God, as to our owne puissance, and thereby provoke his high indignation and displeasure against us.

That, for a man of action, at such a moment, is not in Shakespeare's vein. Piety and humility for the night-time; but "amid the clang of arms," as Mr. Stone says, he would have his hero "speak in a rapture of martial ardor which sweeps every other thought from his mind." Now he must think only of battle and drink delight of battle. Instead of preaching in such an hour or praying, Shakespeare would have him assert himself, let himself go a bit, like, say, George Washington, another hero who sometimes seemed something of a prig and (in popular legend at least) was always the pink of propriety, but who in battle went so far as to break out spontaneously into oaths. "God's will!" cries King Henry, "I pray thee, wish not one man more . . . God's peace! I would not lose so great an honour." Like Nelson at Copenhagen, he "would not be elsewhere for thousands." Like Roland of old, he would not have wound his horn. "The game's afoot," as he cried to his men before Harfleur; his blood is up; and the name of God rises to his lips only in oaths or in the war-cry, "God for Harry, England, and St. George." Like every man of action, when the time of action arrives he thinks of nothing—feels the need of nothing—save to get into it. And in that hour he has no religion but that of the old English adage, "God helps him who helps himself."

Was Henry, then, as some have thought, Shakespeare's ideal? Gervinus and other German critics have declared he was, being the antithesis of Richard II and Hamlet. Some of them have even gone so far as to say that Henry is Shakespeare himself, with his practical genius and well-balanced nature, his taste for the low as well as the lofty, and his sense of humor in the midst of duty—his liking for play when at work. Mr. W. B. Yeats holds just the contrary. Poet of the Celtic twilight, of them that went forth to battle but always fell, he thinks that

Shakespeare infinitely preferred Richard; and that Henry is given the "gross vices and coarse nerves," and "the resounding rhetoric, as of a leading article," which befit a man who succeeds, though his success was really failure. "Shakespeare watched Henry V, not indeed as he watched the greater souls in the visionary procession, but cheerfully, as one watches some handsome spirited horse, and he spoke his tale, as he spoke all tales, with tragic irony." But when Shakespeare—when any popular dramatist—is ironical, we the people must needs know it; or else his popular art has failed him and missed the mark. Here is no evidence of either. Instead of being sly, or insinuating, or pregnant of innuendo, he is more exuberant and enthusiastic than usual; the choruses, which are the authentic voice of the poet himself, put that beyond the peradventure of a doubt. And the likelihood is that Professor Dowden is nearer the truth; Henry V, at least in some measure, approaches Shakespeare's ideal of the practical man, which is not his highest ideal. Shakespeare, no doubt, admired success, though without worshipping it; he himself succeeded, not inconsiderably in his brief two score and ten; but the men he admired most, I daresay, were the finer spirits such as Hamlet, Brutus, or Prospero, whether they succeeded or failed. It was their devotion and gallantry that he admired, not (pessimistically or sentimentally) their devotion and gallantry foiled or thrown away.

It is more to the point to say that Henry is the ideal of England, not Shakespeare's but his country's notion of their hero-king. He is the king that audiences at the Globe would have him be. This is particularly true as regards what we nowadays consider his bragging, his priggishness and cant. The obtrusive morality and piety were expected; for that matter they are like the sort of thing you find in a Speech from the Throne or our American Presidential Thanksgiving proclamations at the present day. Officially, piety has been ever in favor; even in ungodly America ceremonies so diverse as the laying of a corner stone and the conferring of the German degree of Ph.D. are performed in the name of the Father, the Son, and the Holy Ghost; and in the new Assembly of Southern Ireland, I notice, the order is given by the Speaker to "call the roll in the name of God."

And on the Elizabethan stage piety and morality are as inseparable from the ideal king as the crown on his head, the royal "we" in his mouth, or the "strut" (lingering down to the eighteenth century to be admired by Sir Roger de Coverley) with which his royal legs must tread the stage. There is in all Elizabethan dramatic art something naïve—something self-descriptive—in the lines, which in the three centuries of evolution towards the more purely and strictly dramatic has nearly disappeared. The wicked, like Richard III in his first soliloquy, know that they are wicked; the good, that they are good; heroes like Julius Caesar boast and vaunt their prowess; and a king, like a god on the stage, must every minute remember, and make us remember too, that he is nothing less. Henry's preaching, swaggering, and swinging of the scepter may repel us a bit today; but that is because as we read we democratically take him for no more than a man, as people at the Globe did not nor were expected to do. Even we, at the theatre, are perhaps not so different and enlightened as we think. King Edward VII, not emulating the ceremoniousness of his ancestors, walked and talked like other people; but on the stage, not more than a score of years ago, Richard Mansfield, as Henry V, found it expedient to strut and swagger a bit again, in the fashion that pleased Sir Roger.

Or if Henry's blatant piety still offend us, surely we should find relief from it in his bragging and swearing. For these efface any impression of sanctimoniousness—these are royal, too, in the genuine antique style. Fancy William the Conqueror, Richard the Lion-hearted, or a king of Henry of Lancaster's kidney, shorn of all these high privileges and immunities of utterance, particularly on the stage. A medieval king can hardly be expected to talk like a gentleman in top hat and gaiters. The lion must not speak small—leviathan must not speak soft words unto thee—but have his roar. Despite our enlightenment, most of us, I suppose, have a sneaking notion of a king as one who talks and does, with a superlatively grand air, pretty much as he pleases. At the theater— at the Elizabethan theater far more than at ours—many, for the time being, have hardly any other notion of him at all. "We are the makers of manners," says Henry himself. And something of this loftiness and liberty of utterance must be granted him even in his morality and piety.

For through it all the man appears. Like Shakespeare's other characters Henry has an individual tone, his own voice, not just anybody's, and one unmistakably human. It swells and subsides, pulses and undulates, alive as a limb in a Rubens or a Raphael. Here are both man and king, both individual and Englishman, in Henry's mingled downrightness and moderation, as he flings his cards upon the table, though ready enough for all that to play on:

> There's for thy labour, Montjoy.
> Go bid thy master well advise himself,
> If we may pass, we will; if we be hind'red,
> We shall your tawny ground with your red blood
> Discolour; and so, Montjoy, fare you well.
> The sum of all our answer is but this:
> We would not seek a battle, as we are;
> Nor as we are, we say we will not shun it.
> So tell your master.

That's the voice of a king, a man, an Englishman, and yet not quite that of any other that I know. . . .

4.

I am well aware that this interpretation of Henry's character is not that of some eminent recent critics. Like Mr. Yeats, they too think him coarse, hard, cruel, or calculating; and they have the same idealistic contempt for the vulgarity of success, and are likewise addicted to the Celtic cult of failure (though so far as a stranger in these British isles can discover, the Celts themselves, as in America, now worship at a different altar, and their prayers are heard). My interpretation, based upon that of Mr. Stone, is led and regulated by historical considerations of Shakespeare's intention and the prepossessions of his audience; theirs is pretty much as if the play were *not* a popular patriotic spectacle in the days of Elizabeth and the Armada, but came from the pen of Browning, say, or Mr. Drinkwater. They in my opinion thrust Shakespeare out of his play, who in his own person, in the second chorus, calls Henry the mirror of all Christian kings—words which only echo those of his author Holinshed:—"a maiestie was he that both lived and died a paterne in princehood, a lodestarre in honour, and mirror of magnificence, the more highlie exalted in his life, the more deeplie lamented at his death, and famous to the world alwaie." How else, pray, could on an Elizabethan stage the victor of Agincourt have been presented?

The author's intention, here so manifest, is the prime thing for the reader to consider. Even in modern dramas and novels it is; and the writers themselves have often to complain of misapprehension, and in order to forestall it some of them, like Shaw, Barker, and Bataille, take pains to expound their purposes and methods in prefaces or other comments of their own. How much more necessary it is to know and appreciate the purposes and methods of dramatists three centuries old, and to consider whether in our personal judgment of them we are swayed by those prevalent today!

Not that the purpose of the author is everything—he may have failed. And Shakespeare's opinion of Henry may not be borne out by the words and conduct he devises for him in the text. This evidently is the opinion of the critics; or else that Shakespeare really intended him to be coarse, politic, a merely efficient and successful man of the world. Whichever it be, Professor Cunliffe has rightly objected, and has shown that it is owing to our present-day prepossessions—our insensibility to the divinity that doth hedge a king, and our aversion to Henry's religiosity, to his type of coarse sally and practical joke, and to his avowal in soliloquy, of earlier days, in *Henry IV,* that he consorts with his wild companions only as a pastime, in order that he may shine in his virtue the brighter on the throne. But Mr. Cunliffe in turn himself proceeds to interpret him as efficient, though in a better sense. Negatively, Mr. Cunliffe seems to me to be in the right; positively, not wholly so. His quarrel with the contemporary critics appears to be only that they are not favorable. He really takes much the same point of view, uses much the same words, only he blunts their edge. And this is inevitable, because of the position that he has assumed at the outset. "Let us try," he says, "to make out as far as we can how Shakespeare himself conceived [his characters]; but after all the one great question for us is the impression they make on our minds." In fact, Mr. Cunliffe has, whether implicitly or explicitly, stood by Shakespeare's conception in criticizing the opinion of the critics; but wholly by the "impression" in establishing his own.

Both Mr. Cunliffe and the critics have insufficiently considered the conception of the dramatist and his technique, as well as the ethics of the age. The royal strut we have considered above. That, as well as Henry's religiosity and his practical joking, is necessary to the poet's purpose in presenting a truly popular English hero-king: and the expectations of the audience are here at one with earlier dramatic practice and the Renaissance critical principle of "decorum." The "efficiency" is another matter. It is an unpleasant word even as Mr. Cunliffe uses it, something of a euphemism. And this impression that he and the other critics receive is mainly owing to two things: the soliloquy already referred to—

> I know you all, and I will awhile uphold
> Etc.   (*I Henry IV*, I, ii.)

and Henry's treatment of Falstaff. The soliloquy all the critics take psychologically, and rightly they then object to the Prince's sowing wild oats so consciously and cunningly, in order to make his reformation the more telling. That would be unendurable. But really it is only the old-fashioned self-descriptive method that we have spoken of above, which Shakespeare in soliloquy employs both with heroes and with villains. It enlightens and reassures his audience. And if that be so, the other charge, of treason to Falstaff, collapses of itself. Mr. Bradley says that the Prince "should have given Sir John clearly to understand that they must say goodbye on the day of his accession." Then it would have been part of the character, beyond a doubt. And Mr. Cunliffe, in defence of Henry's casting him off, can find nothing better to say for him than that it was "a political necessity and a fore-ordained part of Henry's plan." But in the soliloquy there is no avowal of such a purpose, and when the thing comes about, whether in the play or in Holinshed before that, it is not as a matter of expediency at all but only of morals. To Shakespeare, moreover, Falstaff is not the wholly amiable, well-nigh estimable character that he has since become. The King casts him off with a regrettable priggishness, but not in the spirit of expediency or policy. The King casts him off, but morally, officially it is to his credit. The poet's hand here is a bit too heavy, but he would simply convey to the audience that as King of England Henry has broken with the past.

5.

In *Henry V* the supreme comic figure does not appear; that was a risk not to be taken. The reformed young king could not decorously permit of him in his presence; and, in his presence or out of it, he would have upset the balance, and broken the unity, of the play. So, like Cervantes with Don Quixote, and Addison with Sir Roger de Coverley, he kills him off to keep him from falling into weaker hands. His death is reported, not presented; and that too is well ordered, for the death of a comic character should not touch us too nearly. Here it does not: as it is told by Mrs. Quickly, the pathetic and the comic were never better blended by mortal pen. And the whole little scene is the best thing in the play— whether it be for Falstaff's cronies as they comment and engage in reminiscences, or for the fat knight himself as his shade is thus summoned up before our eyes again.

It is a scene that might easily have become sentimental or maudlin. But sullen and dogged Bardolph is still himself, even in this the one exalted moment of his life: "Would I were with him, wheresome'er he is, either in heaven or in hell!" And motherly, consolatory Quickly, who had always looked on the bright side, and called shady things by fair names, is still herself as she smoothes Sir John's pillow and bids him " 'a should not think of God,—I hoped there was no need to trouble himself with any such thoughts yet." The "fine *end*," she thinks, is all that matters, hell or heaven. And now that he has got to one or the other, she will not have it that he is in hell, but in Arthur's bosom, if ever man went to Arthur's bosom. That British bosom for Abraham's, and not troubling oneself with God till the very pinch of death is at one's throat, are typical of her simple heathen soul. Her own legendary king is more to her than your alien patriarch; superstitition is deeper rooted in her heart than the Christian faith; and the blossoming there is the kindliness of naked and benighted human nature, not of piety. She knows and notes the immemorially ominous signs and seasons—the hour just between twelve and one—even at the turning of the tide—and his fumbling with the sheets, playing with flowers, and smiling upon his fingers' ends. All that she noticed; and still, woman and heathen that she was, she comforted him by bidding him not yet think of God. But the fine end he made justified her—"an it had been any christom child," she said of it —for not having put him to that sore "trouble." For he, a heathen too, who had avoided trouble and endeavored to be "o' good cheer" all his life long, took her comfort readily and thought of God no more. Even the fat knight, though now his nose be sharp as a pen, seems still himself. "Peace, good Doll!" he had said in his latter heyday, "do not speak like a death's-head; do not bid me remember mine end. . . ."

CHARLES WILLIAMS

Henry V

WITH *Henry V,* therefore, Shakespeare reached the climax of exterior life; it is at once a conclusion and a beginning. It is not primarily a patriotic play, for the First Chorus knows nothing of patriotism nor of England, but only of a *Muse of fire which would ascend the brightest heaven of invention* by discovering a challenge between mighty monarchies. Patriotism certainly keeps breaking in, but rather like the army itself: the mass behind Henry is dramatically an English mass, and as the play proceeds he becomes more and more an English king. So much must be allowed to the patriots; it is, however, for them to allow that he becomes something else and more as well, and it is in that something more that his peculiar strength lies.

Before defining that, however, and his own words define it, it may be well to remark a few of the differences between *Henry V* and its precedent *Henry IV.* The newer manner of the blank verse itself is accentuated; it gains in speed. Less even than in *Henry IV* are there any involutions or adornments; its movements, like the action of the persons, admit of no delay. It has lost superfluity, though it has not yet gained analysis. No word blurs, but each word does not yet illuminate, as each was to illuminate in that later play of action and vision, *Antony and Cleopatra.* Here it is equivalent to the King's desire and the King's deed, and equals the one with the other. But there is, at first, no variation between the King and other characters, as there is variation between the Prince and Hotspur and Falstaff in *Henry IV:* what the King is, he is, and the others are apart from him. In fact, the next differences between the two plays are (i) the omission of Hotspur, and (ii) the omission of Falstaff. It will be said that Hotspur is dead before *Henry IV* ends and Falstaff dies soon after *Henry V* begins. But whatever historical necessity or moral convenience compelled those two deaths, the result is to leave the stage free not only for King Henry himself, but for something

From *Shakespeare Criticism: 1919–1935,* ed. A. Bradbey (Oxford, 1936), pp. 180–188. Reprinted by permission of the Clarendon Press.

else—for the development of the idea of honour. In *Henry IV* honour had been peculiarly the property of Hotspur, and it had seemed like being his property in a narrower sense. He had regarded it almost as if it were something he owned as he owned his armour, something that he could capture and possess.

> By heaven methinks it were an easy leap
> To pluck bright honour from the pale-fac'd moon,
> Or dive into the bottom of the deep,
> Where fathom-line could never touch the ground,
> And pluck up drowned honour by the locks;
> So he that doth redeem her thence might wear
> Without corrival all her dignities:

Against this splendid and egotistical figure is the figure of Falstaff. Up to the last act of *2 Henry IV* the distinction of Falstaff had been that, though he may want a lot for his comfort, he does not need it for his complacency. Hotspur, without a sense of his own honour, feels himself deficient; it is why he rebels. Falstaff, without the same sense, feels himself free; it is why he runs away or fights as circumstances and his own common sense dictate. Henry V might have been made like either of them; in fact, he was made like neither. Neither Hotspur nor Falstaff could suit the Muse of fire or the brightest heaven. Honour must for Henry in his own play be something consonant with that brightness, and that invention discovered a phrase which made honour more than reputation—whether for possession or repudiation.

> And those that leave their valiant bones in France,
> Dying like men, though buried in your dunghills,
> They shall be fam'd; for there the sun shall greet them,
> And draw their honours reeking up to heaven,
> Leaving their earthly parts to choke your clime.

Their bodies are dead; their honours live, but not as fame upon earth. The heaven of invention is to suggest this other heaven; the honour of poetry is to show the honour of the spirit in challenge. It is a little reminiscent of *Lycidas;* where also Fame is transmuted into something pleasing to "all-judging Jove." The honours which so live are the spirits and souls of the righteous—anyhow, of the righteous at Agincourt. It is to Henry that the identification is given; it is for him that honour is now a name for man's immortal part. If that venture of war which is the result of the challenge between two great worldly powers, two mighty monarchies, is defeated, this end at least is left to those who carry themselves well in that venture.

As far as the war itself is concerned, the play did not attempt any illusion. It put war "in the round." The causes of it are there; dynastic claims are the equivalent of the modern prestige of governments. The force of the verse carries the sincerity of the intention, and the tennis-balls are part of the cause of the war; that is, the other monarchy is also involved. Any insincerity is part of the way of things, but insufficient to cloud the glory of the change. In this sense Shakespeare threw over the diplomatic advice of the King in *Henry IV* as well as the martial egotism of Hotspur.

Besides the causes of war there is, in the first Harfleur scene, what a soldier-poet called "Joy of Battle"; so, with a horrid faithfulness, in the second Harfleur scene, is the usual result of Joy of Battle. So, finally, in the field before Agincourt, is a kind of summing-up. War is not so very much more dangerous than peace; one is almost as likely to be killed one way as the other. "Every soldier's duty is the King's, but every subject's soul is his own," which if he keep clean, it does not very much matter whether he lives or dies. Death is not all that important—to Henry (who in the play was going to fight), to the lords, to the army, and, as a consequence, to the citizens of Harfleur. The Duke of Burgundy's oration in the last Act describes all the general advantages of peace, but it does not do more. Peace, as a general thing, is preferable to war, but life is pretty dangerous any way—pretty bloody, in every sense of the word—and a healthy male adult should be prepared for death at any moment. So what does it matter? It is not the modern view, but we are not Elizabethans, and our police are efficient.

Honour then—the capacity to challenge the world and to endure the result of challenge—is the state to be coveted.

> But if it be a sin to covet honour,
> I am the most offending soul alive.

Those lines come from the most famous of Henry's speeches. But there is another and much shorter and less famous speech which throws a stronger light on Henry. There had been a minor crisis—the conspiracy in the Second Act—before the great crisis of Agincourt. But as no one has the least interest in the Lord Scroop of Masham, and as no one can feel the King himself has had time to love him behind the scenes either in *Henry IV* or *Henry V,* the conspiracy fails to excite. We are left to listen to the King being merely vocal. When, however, the central crisis approached, Shakespeare had another way of being equivalent to it. This comes in the English camp by night before the battle, very soon after the greatest thing in the play, the sublime Fourth Chorus. In that Chorus a change had been presented as coming over the whole war. The venture had gone wrong, the challenge delivered to the world of the French had been accepted and that French world had trapped the English army and was on the point of destroying it. At the point of that pause the Fourth Chorus delivers its speech, describing the night, the gloom, and the danger. But its speech, if the words are literally fol-

lowed, has two futures. The first is Agincourt; the second is the tragedies. There is not only a change in *Henry V;* there is a still darker
change away from *Henry V*. The Muse of fire has been ascending her
heaven—that is the poetry's own description of what it has been trying
to do. But now it directly suggests that it is doing something quite
different.

> Now entertain conjecture of a time
> When creeping murmur and the poring dark
> Fills the wide vessel of the universe.

The word "universe" means, certainly, earth and heaven in that darkness before the battle. But there seems no reason why it should not
also mean "universe" in the accepted sense, the whole world and the
whole heaven, including the brightest heaven of poetry with which we
began. It is all this which is beginning to be filled with creeping murmur
and the poring dark. Poetry and (so to speak) life are being occupied
by this universal noise and night. It is not yet so fixed; it is but a guess
and a wonder. "Now entertain conjecture—" It is the prelude to all the
plays that were to come.

From poetry thus conceiving of its own probable business, both locally
at Agincourt and universally, and its future, two other enlargements
follow. One concerns the English army; the other, the King.

The *Muse of Fire* is compelled to behold the army as "so many horrid
ghosts," and the description of the soldiers is that of men who are in the
state she has described. It is an army but it is also humanity. To "sit
patiently and inly ruminate the morning's danger" is a situation familiar
enough to us in peace as to them in war, if "danger" also may be given
a wider meaning than that of battle. Illness, unemployment, loneliness,
these are the things that make sacrifices of "the poor condemned English," that make them "pining and pale." It is among such a host of
spectral images of mankind that the King moves, and the Chorus imag-
ines him as their contrast and support: "the royal captain of this ruined
band." It remains true, however, that the Chorus has to do this without
having had, up to that point, much support from the play itself. Henry
has been cheerful and efficient and warlike and friendly, but he has not
suggested to us his capacity for being an almost supernatural "little
touch of Harry in the night." The wider and the darker the night, the
more that gleam shines. But why?

The cause follows. When the King appears he is speaking, more or
less lightly, of the advantages which evil chances bring with them. It is
not a particularly original remark, not a moment of "great insight," and
we need not perhaps suppose it is meant to be solemn or serious. It is
in the next speech that the sudden difference between Henry and all
the rest appears.

> 'Tis good for men to love their present pains
> Upon example; so the spirit is eas'd:
> And when the mind is quicken'd, out of doubt,
> The organs, though defunct and dead before,
> Break up their drowsy grave, and newly move
> With casted slough and fresh legerity.

This is the centre of Henry's capacity. He "loves" his present pains, and his spirit is therefore eased. He has rather more than accepted darkness, danger, defeat, and death, and loves them. It is this which gives him a new quickening of the mind, new motions of the organs; it destroys sloth and the drowsy grave of usual life. It is this love and the resulting legerity of spirit which enable him to be what the Chorus describe, and what the rest of the Act accentuates.

> Upon his royal face there is no note
> How dread an army hath enrounded him;

how can there be when he loves being enrounded?

> But freshly looks and overbears attaint
> With cheerful semblance and sweet majesty.

It is precisely a description of what he has done within himself. Therefore every wretch "plucks comfort from his looks," receiving the "largess universal" from his liberal eye—from the eased spirit, the quickened mind, the moving organs, which are the effect of his love for present pains.

Perhaps this also was something of the explanation of the dead Falstaff; perhaps Henry was more like his old acquaintance than he altogether knew. Only the word "love" can hardly be used of Falstaff in any sense; it was by no accident or haste that Shakespeare could not show him in more "love" than the odd possibility of lechery excites. He enjoyed his dilemmas in the sense that he enjoyed being equal to them, but Henry enjoys them because he is careless of them.

There is a distinction, and it lies in the fact that the King's spirit is "honour" whereas Falstaff's is the rejection of "honour." It also lies in the fact that Falstaff does die when he cannot conquer "the King's unkindness." If ever Falstaff's spirit was drawn reeking up to heaven, he would only enter it on his own terms, but Henry will enter it on Heaven's terms. It is Falstaff's greatness that we are delighted to feel heaven give way to him; Henry's that we are eased by his giving way to heaven. But the artistic difference is that there is no more to be done in the method of Falstaff—he is complete and final. He can be continually varied and repeated, but he cannot be developed. Henry is complete, but not final. For he, in whose honour there is no self-contradiction, could love his pains simply because there was nothing else to do except run away, and that the same honour forbade. The genius of Shakespeare proceeded, however, immediately to imagine an honour in which self-contradiction did passionately exist; it emerged as Brutus, and was set in front of a power which was more "monstrous" than that of the French army; he called that monstrosity Caesar, and made another play out of those other conditions, in which the crisis is a more deeply interior thing, and the heaven of honour begins itself to be at odds.

Henry then has made of his crisis an exaltation of his experience; he has become gay. This gaiety—a "modest" gaiety, to take another adjective from the Chorus—lasts all through the Act. It lightens and saves the speech on ceremony; more especially, it illuminates the speech to Westmoreland. In view of the King's capacity the stress there may well be on the adjective rather than the substantive: "We few, we *happy* few." His rejection of all those who have no stomach for the fight, his offer of crowns for convoy, is part of the same delight: so far as possible he will have no one there who does not love to be there. He makes jokes at the expense of the old men's "tall stories" of the battle, and at the French demand for ransom. We are clean away from the solemn hero-king, and therefore much more aware of the Harry of the Chorus, and of the thing he is—the "touch of Harry in the night." The very last line of that scene —"how thou pleasest, God, dispose the day"—is not a prayer of resignation but a cry of complete carelessness. What does it matter what *happens?*

It is a legerity of spirit, the last legerity before the tragedies. Hamlet was to have a touch of it, but there is little else, in the greater figures, until, as from beyond a much greater distance, it is renewed by a phrase Kent uses of the Fool in *Lear*. Who, says a Gentleman on the moor, is with the King?

> None but the Fool, who labours to outjest
> His heart-struck injuries.

Henry's injuries are not heart-struck; he is no tragic figure. But he deserves more greatly than has perhaps always been allowed. The Muse, *entertaining conjecture* of a new and dreadful world, conjectured also a touch in the night, the thawing of fear, a royal captain of a ruined band, and conjectured the nature of the power of love and consequent lightness that thrills through the already poring dusk.

ARTHUR SEWELL

Character and Society in Shakespeare

CHARACTER AND FALSTAFF

IV

. . . We can only understand Shakespeare's characters so long as we agree that we cannot know all about them and are not supposed to know all about them. They are real for us, but only real to the extent that we have an attitude towards them or make a judgement on them. This is not very different from the manner in which "real" people are real for us, except that with "real" people we bear in mind (if we are wise) that there is a great deal we do not know about them which might, if we knew it, change our attitude and our judgement. In this sense, attitude or judgement in the theatre are prior to "character" and determine its actuality. What, for example, would happen to the play *Othello* if we could know that Iago, like Cassio, muttered in his dreams or could not sleep at nights? Are we certain, once we think of it, that this part of Iago's existence is excluded by anything other than the attitude we take towards him? We are not quite sure whether Iago really meant it when he said that he suspected Othello of having done his office in Emilia's bed; and the uncertainty arises partly from the fact that this is something we must not know about Othello, partly also from the fact that the inner feeling, involved in this, is something we must not know about Iago. There are "rules of evidence" in drama just as there are in a court of law. . . .

It was surely a mistake ever to ask the question: Is Falstaff a coward? Morgann, who first asked it, very rightly made the distinction between the Understanding, which deals in actions, and the Impression made upon us, often at variance with the Understanding. Morgann also affirmed of character-presentation that "just so much is shewn as is requisite, just so much as is impressed": but he went on to say that this "just

From *Character and Society in Shakespeare* (Oxford, 1951), pp. 12–17, 34–37, and 45–52. Reprinted by permission of The Clarendon Press. Subtitles supplied by the present editor. These passages have been abridged.

so much" is able to imply a character which, though "seen in part," may yet be "capable of being unfolded and understood as a whole." He therefore believed it possible to answer the question and proper to put it: Is Falstaff a coward? One might answer that the facts say that he is, but our impression of him, our attitude to him, says that he is not. Falstaff ran away, pretended to be dead; and to do these things was to put the safety of his skin above his human dignity, and this might be thought to be a sort of "cowardice." But not when we are dealing with Falstaff, for Falstaff was very doubtful about "honour," and if we do not believe in "honour" the word "cowardice" has no meaning. Falstaff is not to be judged, as a real person might be judged, in terms of the ordinary moral categories. His running away, his pretending to be dead, his speech on "honour" are all part of his attitude to his world, and it is this that calls from us the ambiguous, even face-saving, judgement of laughter. We do not ask, Was Falstaff a coward? just because we are ourselves infected with Falstaff's notion that perhaps, after all, the question is not so important as we thought it was.

Falstaff is a character, not a real person. What wholeness and consistency he has comes not from within but from the address of his personality *vis-à-vis* his world as it transforms itself into speech and behaviour. The world is his stooge and, so magnanimously does he present himself, he is his own stooge. He subdues and transforms the matter of the moment—even his own monstrous belly—to the purposes of his superlatively comic vision. Such a representation of personality is to be found in a work of art, and its consistency is not psychological but aesthetic. It is the notable distinction of Falstaff's being that he has been conceived quite independently of psychological motivation. His delights, like ours, are aesthetic, even though they have their play in the uncertain world of our moral scruples.

v

Falstaff is aware of his audience, on and off the stage, and the comic artistry is part of the comic character. His life within the play—the only life he has—is a sustained vaudeville turn. The audience is necessary to his being. Nor is he alone of Shakespeare's characters in this. In these characters—they are as various as the melancholy Jaques, Iago, Richard III, Autolycus—we seem to have a high degree of self-awareness which would argue that identification of himself with the character which Coleridge and Keats attributed to Shakespeare. The truth is, however, that in the creation of these persons Shakespeare's identification of himself is not with the character but with the actor. And this identification does not make him ask, What does it feel like to be Falstaff, Iago, Jaques, Richard III? but rather, What effect is Falstaff, Iago, Jaques, Richard III, to make on his audience? A very different matter. This effect is the product of an address to the world, here and now made concrete in the address to the audience.

Each one of these characters has something of the detachment of the artist, and each achieves a satisfaction which has in it an element predominantly aesthetic. From moment to moment they seem to generate a mimesis of their own personalities, and only in the mimesis is the personality really known. They address our moral attitudes and sensibilities, as an artist does, taking their licence for granted, such licence they must have. With them, as with the artist, we give (often through laughter) a temporary permission to a view of life, a questioning of moral conventions, an affirmation of cynical assessments, which—if our neighbour pressed us on the matter—we might well reject. Not only is disbelief in the theatre willingly suspended, but also moral scruples and even accustomed decencies. Both kinds of suspension are necessary to the presentation of character.

This suspension is, of course, never absolute. We give licence as a nobleman may license his fool. We keep our moral scruples and our decencies safely in reserve. Nevertheless, when the character addresses us, he is making a bid for our assent that his attitude, his moral outlook, is more rational than ours. He comes to us, and he asks: "Who is it, then, that says I play the villain?"

VI

Drama, then, through character, prompts us to say: So that is what the world is like, is it? And this or that is the way in which I am recommended to act in my approach to the world? For, after all, vision is not wholly divorced from persuasion. Just as important, perhaps, in the formulation of vision as the way in which certain characters approach their world, is the way in which the world makes its impact on men and women despite themselves. . . . What happens to a person may, in this sense, be just as much "in character" or "out of character" as what the person says or does, and the very probabilities of the play are determined by our attitudes. With Kent, we feel that Lear must die because we would not "on the rack of this rough world stretch him out longer." But we are embarrassed when the king dismisses Falstaff, because our attitude to Falstaff has never included the expectation that his spirits could be so put down. Similarly, the indignities heaped upon Malvolio are almost more than the character can bear. . . .

XV

The view of character here put forward seems to take little account of the fact that Shakespeare's characters awaken in us emotions of pity, contempt, admiration, loathing, and the like, and that in this they can be fruitfully thought of as very real persons. Once we deny in tragedy, for example, our pity for this man's misfortunes, our admiration for some grandeur in his soul, what is left? Is drama really so bloodless that we go to the theatre to become acquainted with a pattern of life-views? In comedy, do we not rejoice that a man has been caught in his folly and has been chastened? In tragedy, do we not witness the spectacle of a man, a particular man, at odds with his fate?

It is the experience of many of us, I fancy, that in the theatre or in the cinema—perhaps after a very good dinner—we have sat with a lump in our throats and tears welling just beneath our eyelids, devoutly hoping that the lights will not go up too soon. Cheap drama, like cheap music, can be curiously potent. And the reason for this seems to be that we are moved by the spectacle of what is happening to this man, this particular man—there, in front of us!—because there is nothing else for us to concern ourselves about. We are at the mercy of the simple stimulus. We are overwhelmed by the tearful situation, because the imagination and the intellect are not otherwise engaged. For the moment, we are debauched.

In Shakespeare's plays, however, what pity we feel, what terror, is of quite a different kind. The stimulus is by no means simple. We have a great deal else to concern ourselves about. And very often, when something like actuality, perhaps unbidden, breaks through, we are at a loss. We become, in fact, at the mercy of the simple stimulus.

I believe that this happens in Shakespeare's final dealings with Falstaff in *Henry IV, Part II*. In general the truly comic character, *qua* comic character, has no interior mode of existence, and what he feels has no relevance in our attitude towards him. Who asks what Falstaff is *feeling*, when he runs away at Gadshill, or counterfeits death at Shrewsbury? Who cares? Are his knees knocking? Do his limbs tremble? Does his heart miss a beat, except for the unusual exercise? Who asks these questions? But, in the end, when the king rejects him, questions of this sort must be asked. At that moment—all the attempts to excuse the king prove this point—we are compelled to ask: What is Falstaff feeling about all this? At last he is brought up to it—a situation which he cannot turn to his own comic purposes, intractable as it is to the subduing magic of personality, his address to the world. This address had never had to reckon with such a moment, and, for the moment, it is quite put down. We are a little ashamed of ourselves. The Falstaff we knew has never asked for our pity. We can do no more than fumble with our sympathies, tell ourselves that it had to be, bear in mind Henry V, justify (or condemn) the king that acts so. And all this because without the transforming power profanity, old age, and surfeit-swelling are no other than themselves, and we had thought them otherwise. We have to treat Falstaff—with what loss!—as a real person. We pity this fat old man; but we cannot say "The pity of it!" And it is only when we pity and can also say, enlarging the moment in its significance, "The pity of it!" that pity is more than self-indulgence. Unless what happens to the character is a mode of bringing together into more poignant relationship the character's way of meeting his world and the comprehensive vision of the play, the character becomes no other than a "real person," and we may be affected more, but moved less. The emotion, like the incident which arouses it, should be a catalyst by means of which vision is released and enriched, so that the particular case is apprehended in terms of the general case of Man.

We suffer something of the same kind of embarrassment in the discomfiture of Shylock and Malvolio.

A different but equally interesting case is found in *Two Gentlemen of Verona*. It is the rule in comedy that characters shall run true to type, that they should behave according to their "humours," that we should know where we are with them. When Proteus, friend of Valentine and lover of Julia, discovers his new affection for Silvia, Valentine's lady, we are presented with a moral crisis outside the realm of the particular comic vision. Proteus loses identity, becomes no more than a "real person," and we do not know what to make of him. The moral crisis, so posed, is prose sediment in the poetry, and the judgement we must make on Proteus is a prose judgement, having nothing to do with the poetry. . . .

CHARACTER IN THE HISTORIES

XVIII

It is easy to reduce Shakespeare's treatment of kingship to the prose of politics, and many critics have done so. But there is one problem in Shakespeare's representation of kings which is not susceptible of this kind of treatment, for it is the indisputable work of poetry and has nothing to do with prose. This is his portrayal of royalty. Richard II is royal, even though as man he forfeits his right to be king. He is always "royal Richard." Henry Bolingbroke, as king, having usurped that kingdom, skilled in policy and carrying ruling authority in his mere presence, is never royal. It is Richard's tragedy that, royal as he shows himself to be, he should look for a flight of angels when he should have collected an army of men. And Bolingbroke, having no privilege as the Lord's Anointed, wins a temporal power through his command of men. And yet—such is the authority of true royalty in the vision of the play— when Richard is left without angels or men we almost feel him to have been deprived of his own. Royalty has its unmistakable style and reveals itself as certainly as greatness of soul in a work of art. It is the style in which a particular address to the world, a royal address, is transformed into poetry, and I dare say, unmistakable as it is, and absolutely unmistakable in Henry V, it defies analysis. Young Arthur has it, when he pleads with Hubert. Royalty does not exempt a man from stupidity or even from wickedness; it alone does not qualify a man to rule his kingdom. But for Shakespeare political order was something more than temporal, and was not to be explained in the handbook. There was in it a mystical element, which not prose but only poetry could represent, and a part of this element is royalty.

The histories are concerned with rebellion, usurpation, conspiracy, and war. These events are hatched in the minds of men and are exercised by the purposes of men. Certainly the idea of Fate is present in the histories, and we are continually reminded of historic expiation and retribution. But these are represented as involved with the moral nature of man, and this moral nature is apprehended in terms of its political manifestations. So it is that character is created. Shakespeare quickens the historic names with those turbulences of spirit which made them dangerous, and he represents the impact of these characters on political order. And once again the impact cannot be represented merely in terms of the prose of politics (though this is a part of the matter), nor can it be represented in terms of the psychology of the rebel. Poetry has other modes of understanding. Political order and political disorder, and those workings of man's moral nature which generate them, are all apprehended together, implying and involved with each other. Henry V is not the reconstruction of a political theorist; he is a poet's representation of a king.

Naturally, then, the studies in loyalty and in treachery are neither simply studies in the psychological make-up of men nor simply excursions into political theory in dramatic form. In *Richard II* the Duke of York shows how difficult loyalty can be. But the difficulty does not chiefly lie in him; it lies in the nature of political order itself, shaping itself, as it must, in the authorities and the obediences of men. His dilemmas are implicit in all political purpose. Nor is it forgotten that in such a commitment there are personal as well as public obligations. At the other pole, rebellion is seen in Shakespeare's histories as a many-headed restlessness within the political order, which threatens to disrupt it, but which, at the same time, is very often a corruption and misdirection of energies which might have made that order fruitful and virtuous. We do not see proneness to rebellion simply as the headsman sees it. We see it sometimes as coming from some address to the world which, in an imperfect political order, finds only in rebellion its satisfaction and exercise. Political order is such that, while much that is evil threatens it, much that is good cannot be contained within it. And so Northumberland finds himself in the same camp with Hotspur, Hotspur with

Glendower, Glendower with Worcester. All these characters are individualized with superb art in terms of Shakespeare's presiding vision of that complex of moral activities which shapes and diversifies political order.

History is more than chronicled events, and more than its abstracted economic and political causes. To make drama out of it, as Shakespeare does, is to recognize that

> Time present and time past
> Are both perhaps present in time future,

and even—for Shakespeare comes nearly to it!—that we are all members one of another. It is perhaps in the women of the play that this element in Shakespeare's vision finds most poignant representation. When they mourn a father or a husband murdered, a son in exile, or a brother solitary in some distant dungeon, they mourn—like the women of Troy, weeping amongst the fallen towers of Ilium—not for themselves alone. In them succeeding generations cry out against the act; it is their wombs which know the bitterness of loss. The Duchess of Gloucester in *Richard II* speaks not only for herself and not only of present property, but for her ancestors and her progeny and of a long heritage, when she complains that what was once a goodly home is now

> But empty lodgings and unfurnish'd walls,
> Unpeopled offices, untrodden stones.

And later in the play the Duchess of York speaks not only of her son, but of sons that might have been her son's, when she asks the Duke, who is about to denounce Aumerle:

> Have we more sons? or are we like to have?
> Is not my teeming date drunk up with time?
> And wilt thou pluck my fair son from my age,
> And rob me of a happy mother's name?

In this way the women of the histories, too, are individualized, and derive their identity, within Shakespeare's poetic vision of political order. How this order is addressed to them (but they are a part of it), what it makes of their world, how the "pattern" is sustained in their suffering, if not in their action—all this is embodied in the women of the histories and gives them their poignant actuality.

The histories raise the problem of character-presentation in a special form. The persons in these plays, whether taken from Plutarch or Holinshed, had had already, before Shakespeare dealt with them, their particular life in men's imaginations. They were known as treacherous or ambitious; their policies had brought them victory or had come to nothing; for kings and counsellors they were famous predecessors and known examples. The audience had already formed some attitude to these characters, and, of course, this attitude was largely determined by the contemporary idea of political order. We may be sure that Shakespeare accepted these attitudes, even though he enriched and energized them. There is a sort of so-called historical play which plays tricks with such set attitudes, as in Bernard Shaw's *Caesar and Cleopatra,* and even in his *Saint Joan.* But the attitudes have to be presumed, otherwise the tricks would never come off. Shakespeare, without playing tricks, can take very good advantage of such a character: as of Hal, in his treatment of Falstaff or in the situation of Henry V's wooing, or, more movingly, in the talk with the common soldiers on the eve of Agincourt. We should remember, however, that even in these more private moments a public, a political character is being represented. It is as though a play about Mr. Winston Churchill should show him laying bricks, giving the V sign to a crowd of women workers, and talking to the survivors of a torpedoed destroyer. Every moment is, in its own way, an image of man in political society and in these moments the character is conceived. Into the political world the study of character, however humane and individual, is extraverted.

How then is character active in the historical plays? Over all, as the presiding vision, there is a poet's idea of political order about which Shakespeare leaves us in no doubt. In *Richard II* the gardener develops the analogy between the state and the garden:

> We at time of year
> Do wound the bark, the skin of our fruit-trees,
> Lest, being over-proud in sap and blood,
> With too much richness it confound itself:
> Had he done so to great and growing men,
> They might have lived to bear and he to taste
> Their fruits of duty; superfluous branches
> We lop away, that bearing boughs may live:
> Had he done so, himself had borne the crown,
> Which waste of idle hours hath quite thrown down.

In *Henry V,* in another comparison, Shakespeare sees political society in the honey-bees, who teach "the act of order to a peopled kingdom." The significance of the vision expressed in these analogies in its relation to character is unmistakable. This vision, as it were, gets to know itself more concretely and more variously in such characters as Bolingbroke, Hotspur, Henry V, and Falstaff. The primary activity of character is apprehended as shaping or mis-shaping political order. And we should note that political disapproval does not imply an absolute disapproval. The bark of the tree must be wounded

> Lest, being over-proud in sap and blood,
> With too much richness it confound itself.

There is no simple opposition of sheep and goats in the internecine tensions of political society. But the political judgement, sometimes sadly enough, must override all others. I do not think that even Falstaff—setting aside his dismissal by the king—is exempt from the presiding judgement; and from that judgement he really derives his astonishing vitality. What, after all, is his speech on Honour? It is the spoken indignation of the individual in revolt against those irksome moral obligations which political order must impose. But, laugh as we may, we do not shuffle those obligations off, and we laugh because we cannot shuffle them off.

It is a consequence of all this that, in general, the characters of the historical plays have no truly private emotions. What inner feeling they may be thought to have is *public emotion*. When Henry IV complains of his sleeplessness the emotion is, as it were, a show. When Richard II takes a handful of English earth in his hands and weeps over it, the action and the feeling belong not to his private but to his public life. Even when Henry V walks round the English camp in the darkness and speaks to the common soldiers, what he says as man enlarges what he is as king.

The imagery in the historical plays has an important part in determining in what world—and in what manner—these emotions are felt. It is imagery which finds the equivalents for emotion in the world of public and political behaviour, and so this emotion takes a relevant part in our imaginative apprehension of political order.

> Why, rather, sleep, liest thou in smoky cribs,
> Upon uneasy pallets stretching thee,
> And hush'd with buzzing night-flies to thy slumber,
> Than in the perfumed chambers of the great,
> Under the canopies of costly state,
> And lulled with sounds of sweetest melody?

In such a way—this is a simple example—is the treatment of character subordinate to the comprehensive vision of the play, and in the presentation of character we are at all times reminded by the imagery of the political society to which character belongs.